Megan Breedlove

MANNA for Moms

God's Provision for Your Hair-Raising,
Miracle-Filled Mothering Adventure

Regal

From Gospel Light
Ventura, California, U.S.A.

Published by Regal
From Gospel Light
Ventura, California, U.S.A.
www.regalbooks.com
Printed in the U.S.A.

Library of Congress Cataloging-in-Publication Data
Breedlove, Megan.
Manna for moms : God's provision for your hair-raising, miracle-filled mothering ad-
venture / Megan Breedlove.
p. cm.
Includes bibliographical references.
ISBN 978-0-8307-5763-3 (trade paper)
1. Mothers—Prayers and devotions. 2. Motherhood—Religious aspects—Christianity—
Meditations. I. Title.
BV4847.B68 2011
242'.6431dc22
2010049149

Rights for publishing this book outside the U.S.A. or in non-English languages
are administered by Gospel Light Worldwide, an international not-for-profit ministry.
For additional information, please visit www.glww.org, email info@glww.org, or write
to Gospel Light Worldwide, 1957 Eastman Avenue, Ventura, CA 93003, U.S.A.

To order copies of this book and other Regal products in bulk quantities,
please contact us at 1-800-446-7735.

With humble gratitude, I dedicate this book to the following:

*My husband, Phil. Words can't possibly convey my thanks to you.
You've supported and encouraged me in every way in beginning our
website, attending writing conferences, and making this book a reality.
You're a wonderful husband to me and father to our children.
I love you, and I'd marry you all over again.*

*My children: Ellie, Kenny, Lindsey and Jessica. You're the best kids
any mom could hope for. I feel blessed every moment of every day to
have you. Thanks for letting me share your stories with others.
I hope that one day, when you're married with children of your own,
you will read this book and hear God's voice speaking to you.
He loves you with all His heart, and so do I.*

Contents

Acknowledgments

It is truly a privilege to thank the following people, each of whom had a significant part in the ministry of bringing this book to print:

Melisa Norcross, my dear friend and a lovely mom of God. You were the first one to suggest, "Hey, maybe you should write a book of devotions."

Tonya Sakowicz, a precious friend and beautiful mom of God, for being among the first to encourage me to *do* something about getting a book published, and for vetting some of my devotions.

The lovely, godly mommies of the October 2004 Babies Christian Mommies thread on BabyCenter.com. Your encouragement regarding the devotions I posted there was more a part of this process than you know.

Renae Brumbaugh, author. Your professional advice and graciousness started me on the road to making my dreams a reality.

The Rev. Dr. R. William Dickson. Because of your Greek class, I now have a greater understanding of and appreciation for Scripture, which greatly influenced the writing of this book. Who knows how many lives you have touched for eternity?

Nancy Komatsu. You theologically vetted my material (before I sent it to my editor) in a thoughtful, gracious manner that honored our Lord (and you know what a split infinitive is!).

My church family—especially the moms!—at Southfield Christian Fellowship. You walk with me as we journey in Christ together, and you let me learn from you. I'm so blessed to call you my friends and sisters.

My mom, Ruth Sheets. You always believed in me, and you told me so. Your encouragement has meant more than you know.

My mother-in-love, Elna Breedlove. Thank you for not only raising an incredible son, but also for loving me as your own, and for encouraging me in this process, and in everything.

My sister, Kristen Lovely; Lori Schmidtke; and Renee Isaac. You're right there in the trenches with me, and you're the best friends anyone could ask for!

Steve Lawson, editor extraordinaire, and the wonderful team at Regal. You all made this book happen, and not only that, you made it the best it can be. Steve, your sense of humor made the whole process much easier (I'll write that giraffe devotional someday).

Almighty God—Father, Son and Holy Spirit. Any gift I have is Yours, and I offer back to You only what I have received. Thank You for blessing me with the means to help others know You. Best of all, thank You for loving me beyond measure. You're incredible.

Introduction

My life can basically be divided into two major eras: B.C. (Before Children) and A.D. (After Delivery). That's because on the day my first child was born, everything changed.

I did my best to anticipate and prepare for the myriad changes I knew were coming. I bought a container of Dreft to wash those delicate baby clothes in, I organized the nursery, and I figured that any other problems could be taken care of during all the free time I would have as a stay-at-home mom. (Okay, so I was a little naïve.)

When my precious daughter Ellie was born, all of these changes took place and more. I was able to cope reasonably well with most of them, even the unanticipated ones. For example, I discovered that now I *really* enjoyed shopping, because people would stop me and tell me how beautiful my baby was—which I was completely certain was true.

But there was one change in particular that I had not foreseen and to which I had some difficulty adjusting. That change came in the area of my quiet times with the Lord. In the B.C. part of my life, I had regular quiet times that followed a particular routine (I'm not saying everyone has to have a routine, but it worked for me). Those moments with the Lord were sweet times for just the two of us. Now it had become the three of us, and I couldn't seem to figure out how to spend time alone with God.

I tried to get up early and have my quiet time, but I was too exhausted. I tried to stay up late, but I started falling asleep. I tried to plan a time during the day, or simply to seize the moment, but babies have an infallible sense of timing. Whenever I tried to sit down and have a quiet time, Ellie suddenly needed me.

I wanted to hear from God—I *needed* to hear from Him more than ever—but I couldn't figure out how to do so. I was frustrated. I was confused. Until, faithful as always, God stepped in.

"Why would you think your quiet time will still look the same?" He said. (He didn't use an audible voice, but I knew what He meant.) *"You need to learn to listen differently."*

Listen differently? I don't get it, God. What do you mean?

"I mean you need to learn to hear My voice in your daily life. I can speak to you all day long. Open your ears, and you will come to hear Me in ways you've never heard Me before.

I still didn't know exactly what God meant, but it sounded good. Besides, it was His command. So I tried it. Do you know what I found? God did, indeed, speak all day long—not *despite* the circumstances of my mothering, but *through* them. He used the ordinary things of my day to illustrate what He wanted to say to me. It's kind of like the way Jesus used parables when He walked this earth. By using the common, ordinary stuff of life such as seeds, harvests and sheep, Jesus communicated spiritual truth to His listeners. God doesn't use the same kinds of things to speak to me (probably because I don't know much about any of those things), but He does use things like racquetballs, candy canes and green bean plants.

The great news is that God wants you to hear His voice, too. Your busyness in mothering is not a barrier to God's reaching your mind and heart. He knows exactly what to say to you and me to get our attention, and when and how to say it.

I once read a famous quote that went something like this: "It took my not having an hour with God to realize that I had all day with Him." You have all day with Him, too. Just because you don't have a solid hour to sit down and have a formal quiet time doesn't mean you can't hear from God as you carry out the calling He's given you. In fact, quite the opposite! He'll speak to you all day long, if you just have ears to hear.

Come with me, and let's journey through some stories of the ways God has spoken to me as I mothered. My prayer is that by reading them, you'll realize that you don't have to rush through bath time so you can go be with God, or get dinnertime conversation out of the way so you can hear His voice. You can hear God *during* bath time, diaper changing time, or measuring cough medicine in the middle of the night. In fact, He is using those very things to speak His love and truth to you.

I pray that He'll open your ears—and mine, too—to hearing His precious voice above the other voices clamoring for our attention.

I pray we'll both learn to really hear Him—even when He speaks in unexpected ways or at unscheduled times. After all, I don't want to miss a single thing He has to say. I know you don't, either.

Megan Breedlove

MANNA
for Moms

1

More "Cratching"

There aren't many things more relaxing than lying back, feet propped up, with a sleeping baby sprawled on top of you. (Okay, maybe lying on a beach lounge in Cancun by myself with the sun warming my back and gentle waves beckoning me into the crystal-clear waters. But I'm talking about things that might actually have a chance of happening.) There's just something about your child's sweet, warm body lying so trustingly against yours that sends love (and hormones) coursing through your veins and makes you feel like all's right with the world.

Jessica loves to lie on me like this. Even though she's two now, she still loves to relax completely against Mama. She especially enjoys it when I "cratch" (her word for "scratch") her back gently. The other day, we were cuddling, and I was feeling pretty relaxed myself. I scratched her for a while and then allowed my fingers to slow down and stop. I thought I had put her to sleep. But just as I lifted my hand from her back, Jessica mumbled sleepily, "More cratching."

Of course she hadn't pronounced the word properly, but I still knew what she wanted. I granted her request.

I'm glad God doesn't require perfect speech from us when we address Him. In fact, with God, there is no such thing as perfect speech. What God cares about is our heart. We can use the most flowery language ever heard and still fail to reach God's heart if our own heart isn't right toward Him. Or we can use language as simple as a two-year-old's and connect immediately and passionately with God's heart.

Of course, it's also possible the other way around. Simple language can fail, and beautifully written language can connect us with God in a way that very few other things can. My point is that we don't have to address God in a certain manner for Him to hear us. We would actually be pretty arrogant to think we can cause God to hear us by praying in a certain way. Some of Jesus' strongest condemnation was for the Pharisees, who thought they were better than everyone else because they knew how to do religion better. They loved to pray long and loud so everyone could see and hear them. And in their prayers, they made speeches not about God's glory, but about how righteous they considered themselves to be. In the parable of the Pharisee and the tax collector, Jesus clearly stated that what impresses God is not someone's manner of praying, but the person's heart (see Luke 18:9-14).

It's really easy to get caught up in making sure we pray properly. In fact, as a person who likes to figure out what the rules are for everything so that I can satisfy them to perfection, it's frustrating to me that there's not one "right" way to pray. I've tried all kinds of acrostics, prayer books and well-meaning suggestions for how to improve my prayer life. Each of those has helped to one extent or another. But after trying all kinds of systems, I have *experienced* the truth that formerly I only knew intellectually—there really isn't only one right way to pray. Whatever system I use, whatever words I use, shouldn't be an end in themselves; they should be the means for expressing my heart to God.

But what if we don't know what's in our heart to express? What if we're stuck not only on the words but also on the content?

That's going to happen sometimes. Some of my most meaningful and worshipful prayer times have been when I simply bowed my heart before God and said nothing as I remained there in His presence. In fact, the Bible tells us that when we don't know how to pray or what to ask, the Spirit Himself intercedes for us with groans that words cannot express (see Rom. 8:26). When we don't know how to pray, God Himself prays for us! How amazing is that?

So let's stop worrying about what we're going to say when we go to God in prayer. Let's put our greater efforts into making sure our heart is right before Him. If we're aware of unconfessed sin, let's confess it. If we know there's some problem but aren't sure what exactly, let's ask Him. And if we think everything's just fine between us and God, let's humbly ask the Holy Spirit to search our heart and reveal to us anything we might be missing.

Then, with our heart in right relationship to God, we'll be in a position to receive the greatest spiritual blessing there is—communion with God Himself. Of primary significance will be the fact that we're in God's presence. Words will fade into secondary importance.

In the same way, the Spirit helps us in our weakness. We do not know what we ought to pray for, but the Spirit himself intercedes for us with groans that words cannot express.

ROMANS 8:26

REFLECTION QUESTIONS

1. Do you ever get caught up in trying to pray "right"? Are you relieved to know there's more than one "right way" to pray?

2. If you were to think about presenting yourself before God with no plan for how to proceed, and simply let His Spirit move your heart in the direction you should pray, how would you feel? Why not try it?

2

Racquetball as a Shower Sport

I love playing racquetball . . . except when I'm in the shower.

Actually, until yesterday, I never thought of racquetball as a shower sport. Every Monday I go to the YMCA to meet a friend, and we play as many games as we can squeeze into two hours. Not once during any of those games have I thought, *Hey, I bet this would be really fun to play while I'm standing in the tub.*

But the other day when I was taking my shower, with Jessica playing nearby (I can never take a shower anymore without a kid or two—or three or four—in the bathroom with me), I heard a strange, bouncy kind of sound. I started to turn and search for the source of the sound, but I didn't need to. It came rolling toward my feet in the form of one of my blue racquetballs.

I pulled back the curtain to see two-year-old Jessica standing there, grinning as if she had just done something hilarious.

"Jessica, did you throw a racquetball in the shower with Mommy?" I asked.

"Uh-huh," she said proudly. "Give it back."

"Silly girl," I said, handing the ball to her.

I closed the shower curtain and turned toward the spray of water, only to hear—yep, you guessed it—*boing, boing, boing*. I waited for the ball to stop bouncing before I took a step. I didn't want to have to try to explain that one to an ER doc—"Yeah, um, I fell on a racquetball in the shower. No, really."

Again I handed the ball back, and again, a few seconds later, it bounded back into the tub. Jessica and I repeated this routine three or four times until I was spending more time playing racquetball than getting clean.

"Okay, that's enough," I said, returning the ball for what I hoped would be the last time.

My shower time hadn't turned out the way I had envisioned. I thought I would get in there, get clean, get out and get ready for my day. I know, I know, I was naïve. You'd think that with four kids, I would know better. Yet despite my years of experiencing the developmental stages of a child's behavior, Jessica had come up with an idea that surprised me.

No matter how many children we have or how many years we've been a mom, we can never anticipate everything. If you've ever met a mom who seemed to be able to take anything in stride, well, she may have been able to do so, but I guarantee you, she was surprised by some of it.

Actions, emotions and circumstances will all take us by surprise. There's just no way around that. Just when we think we have this mothering thing all figured out, circumstances will change or our child will do something she's never done before.

But there's really no need to know everything, like we sometimes think there is. It's Satan's lie that we are the ones ultimately responsible for our children's upbringing.

Satan knows very well what you and I don't often think about: God is the one who's responsible for our kids. So one of Satan's favorite strategies is to convince us that *we* are the ones who have to make sure everything comes out right, to provide every opportunity for our children and ensure their safety at every turn. Satan loves it when we try to take God's job upon ourselves, because it means we are no longer relying on God—who will most certainly succeed—but on ourselves, who are certain to fail.

Yes, we should do everything we can for our children. We must be vigilant about their safety, diligent to teach them God's Word, and creative in offering them opportunities to have fun and grow. But we're supposed to do all these things in God's strength and while drawing upon His wisdom, not while relying on our own limited resources.

It's like when a two-year-old wants to put on her own clothes. She struggles mightily—tugging, pulling, crying. "Do you want me to help you?" her parent asks.

"I do it myseff!" she shouts. (Ask me how I know.)

If she would only accept her parent's help, she'd be able to do the job better and more thoroughly. Yet, she struggles on.

The same is true about us. We have all of God's resources at our disposal, yet we refuse to draw upon them or we simply never think about it. Yes, our two-year-old must one day learn to get dressed on her own. But in our mothering, we will never be alone. God is always right there in it with us.

So if you think you're not very creative, or you're concerned that you don't know enough about parenting, or you're afraid you're just one step away from making a serious mistake, remember this: God loves your child even more than you do. And He's ready to help you any time you need it, if you just ask.

Why? Because He loves your child, and He loves you. And that means He won't leave you alone in this crazy, joyous, messy adventure called mothering.

If any of you lacks wisdom, [she] should ask God, who gives generously to all without finding fault, and it will be given to [her].
JAMES 1:5

REFLECTION QUESTIONS

1. Does it sometimes frustrate you or even threaten to drive you crazy that kids can be so unpredictable? How might you learn to rejoice in this fact instead?

2. Are you quick to ask for God's wisdom in your parenting? If not, why not?

3

Spiritual Sunlight

You've never seen a boy as proud of a green bean plant as my son was of his.

Kenny brought home a small, disposable, rinse-the-toothpaste-out-of-your-mouth-sized cup of dirt from our homeschool co-op, assuring me it had a seed inside. I asked him to let me keep it safe for him on the way home. While my kids got into the van, I loaded their paraphernalia—including the seed cup—into the van. And in so doing, like any good mommy would have, I managed to spill a good bit of the precious dirt on the floorboard.

Kenny was in the back of the van in his booster seat, so he hadn't seen me, and I didn't confess my misdeed. I simply scooped up as much of the dirt as I could, hoping the seed was still somewhere in the cup instead of under the floor mat. I drove home with the cup secured, praying that somehow, something would grow out of that cup that Kenny would be proud of.

Little did I know that God was about to answer my prayer in abundance.

I set the cup on the kitchen windowsill and made sure to keep the dirt moist over the next couple days. I know, it was Kenny's plant, and he should have watered it himself; but after almost ending the seed's short life before it began, I felt responsible for it. So I watered it, and Kenny checked every day to see whether it was growing. Then, one day . . .

"Mommy! My green bean plant is growing!" Kenny's excitement was boundless. He made sure that each of his sisters knew it was growing, and he urged them to come look at it. Each day, he watched and marveled as that plant grew taller.

Thank You, God, I prayed, breathing a huge sigh of relief.

After a few days, I suggested we move Kenny's plant to the front porch, where it could get better sunlight. Kenny, being very protective of it, wasn't sure we should do that. After all, the plant seemed to be doing fine on its own. I explained to him that direct sunlight would be good for it. "It'll help your plant grow," I promised.

"Then let's move it!" Kenny agreed.

We placed the cup on a little table on the porch, and Kenny made sure it had just the right spot to receive what he deemed the proper amount of sunlight. It was hard for me to get him back inside and away from his treasure, but somehow, I managed.

The next morning, before I was even fully awake, Kenny ran into my bedroom, begging me to let him go outside and check on his green bean plant. He diligently checked on it each morning without being reminded, and each morning he was amazed. "Mommy! Come *see!*" he shouted excitedly, and I always rushed outside to admire the new growth.

One morning, as Kenny and I admired his plant, I suggested that he show it to Daddy. Kenny eagerly went to find Daddy and lead him outside. "Oh, wow, it's growing!" my husband said, sounding suitably impressed.

"The reason why it growed is because it got some sunlight," Kenny said confidently.

He was right. But the principle of growth that Kenny discovered applies to a lot more than green bean plants. It applies to our children and to us as well.

Put simply, when we get the right kind of light, we grow.

Sufficient sunlight is certainly helpful to our physical bodies. I'm convinced that kids grow faster in the summer months, partly because of all the time they spend playing outside. But even more important to our growth is the light of God's presence and His Word in our hearts and minds.

Too often, we mommies get so busy caring for our families and running our homes that we fail to immerse ourselves in fellowship with God and His Word. Expecting to grow spiritually without spending time in the Word on a regular basis is about as realistic as expecting a green bean plant to grow without light. It just can't happen.

The Bible makes it abundantly clear that only God can grow us spiritually. We can't grow ourselves. So if we're not in touch with Him through prayer and His Word, how will we grow at all?

Most of us don't have long, uninterrupted stretches of time to devote to prayer or Bible study. Many times, we have to take whatever time we can get, whenever we can get it. And that's okay. God understands a mom's busy schedule, and He can grow us even when the time we spend with Him doesn't look like we think maybe it should. He can show us what time spent with Him will look like in our own life.

But we have to desire to come to Him. He usually won't force His way into our daily lives and demand that we face Him. But if our relationship with Him ever gets cold enough that forcing us to pay attention to Him is the only way He can get us to do so—well, I can guarantee that's a situation none of us really wants to be in.

So let's make sure we don't neglect our own spiritual growth in the busyness of tending to our children. After all, God should still come first in our lives. Let's give Him the place He rightly deserves: first place, even before our families. Putting God first doesn't take anything away from our families. In fact, it's quite the opposite, because one of the best things we can give them is a mom who knows and loves God.

Oh, and we should probably offer them green beans sometimes too.

So neither he who plants nor he who waters is anything,
but only God, who makes things grow.
1 CORINTHIANS 3:7

REFLECTION QUESTIONS

1. Are you growing spiritually? Do you spend enough time in God's Word? If not, why not?

2. If you don't, what could you do to resolve some of these factors so that you give priority to time spent in God's Word?

4

The Best Cake Ever

I enjoy making my children's birthday cakes. I don't make them from scratch; my kids seem to be happy enough with going to the store to pick out a mix ("I want *that* one! With the sprinkles!"). But I do enjoy making different sized cakes in the pan, cutting and arranging the pieces just so, and frosting and decorating them for that magical effect that transforms them into whatever character or theme my child likes that year.

When Ellie turned four, I made her a castle cake. It had several layers in varying sizes. It was festooned with pink frosting, a million kinds of candy, some sugar cones placed upside down and coated with pink sugar (the turrets), and little flags waving from the tops (bottoms, actually) of the sugar cones. It would have been a great cake, except that it looked like the Leaning Castle of Pisa.

And it seemed to lean in multiple directions. Now that's quite an accomplishment, mind you. Not everyone can make and decorate a cake where the layers of the castle slant at least two different directions and the turrets a third. It was clear that my castle needed some serious foundation work.

Several cakes later, with more experience under my belt, I know what I should have done differently. But at the time, I gazed bewilderedly at the giant, sloping mound of pink, sugar-covered goo, and I thought, *This is* not *a good cake*. I knew everyone would realize I had made it, since it was obvious I hadn't bought it from a professional. Realistically speaking, it wasn't a *bad* cake. It just looked . . . well . . . amateurish, and I wanted a perfect cake for my daughter's party. I wanted a castle fit for a princess.

But what was I going to do? There was no time left for a second attempt. The party was about to start. I sighed and squared my shoulders. I would just have to be brave, show my daughter her cake, and explain that it hadn't come out quite the way I intended. Then I'd apologize and hope she wouldn't be too disappointed.

"Um . . . Ellie?" I called. "Come see your cake."

I stood next to the stove where I'd balanced the cake platter. I would take ownership of this cake even if it wasn't perfect. Ellie ran in, her little curls bouncing, and came to an abrupt halt as she spotted my creation. Her mouth dropped open. "Wow! That's the most beautiful cake ever!" she exclaimed.

"It *is*?"

"Yeah! It's really beautiful!" she exclaimed, and ran off to play.

I took another glance at the cake to make sure that she and I were both looking at the same cake. I looked it up and down, over and around. It was still leaning to the right like crazy. The frosting wasn't quite smooth, and one of the flags had fallen off the sugar-cone turret.

But this time, seeing it with my daughter's eyes, I beheld beauty.

This time, I saw a huge, multi-layered home fit for a princess, festooned with enough candy to fill a candy store. Sugar sparkled from the turrets, and the flags waved in an imaginary breeze. Plus, the whole thing was covered with pink icing, and what could be better or more delicious than that?

That's when I realized something: God thought my cake was beautiful too. He knew I'd put my best effort into it and made it with love. As far as He was concerned, *that* was what determined its beauty, not the perfection of my technique.

I must admit that I tend to see mostly the imperfections in what I do. For example, I'll know the house looks better than it did before I started cleaning, but all I see are the six piles of laundry still spread out in the laundry room. Or I'll know the children enjoyed supper, but what stands out to me is the fact that I didn't serve them any vegetables.

Fortunately, God is not nearly as critical of my performance as I am. Whenever I remember that, my soul sighs in relief. True, God has a standard of complete holiness, and anything less than that is sin. But I'm referring here to those times when there's no moral issue involved. When I answer to God for how I lived today, He's not going to ask me if I kept the neatest, most well-appointed house in the world and had the best-behaved children. He's going to ask me if I built our home the best I could and loved my children with all my heart.

My cake would never have made the front cover of *Amazingly Perfect, Professional-Looking (Despite the Fact that You Made It at Home) Birthday Cakes*. But I believe that when God saw that Leaning Castle of Pisa, in all its glorious, gooey pink imperfection, He saw love. He saw my heart for my daughter. And He knew that while there might be more technically perfect castle cakes in the world, there couldn't be one made with more love.

So in His eyes, my cake was just perfect.

The LORD does not look at the things man looks at. Man looks at the outward appearance, but the LORD looks at the heart.

1 SAMUEL 16:7

REFLECTION QUESTIONS

1. Do you tend to look at results, or at how hard someone (including you!) tried, and the attitude of the person's heart?

2. What difference might it make in your personal life and home life if you began to concentrate on your family's heart attitudes and left the results to God?

5

Juggling Monkeys

When you are the mom of more than one young child, getting them anywhere can be a little crazy. You know what I mean. Even when the kids are behaving well, life is just a little bit wild, and things that used to be no problem in your pre-child days are now mind-bogglingly difficult. For example, going out to eat.

First, you have to get all of your children into the minivan. Child #1 heads out the door before you're ready, because, after all, *she's* ready; child #2 follows child #1; child #3 is whining to be picked up; and child #4, already strapped into the infant carrier, has just made a really fragrant diaper that you're certain other diners would notice.

So your husband goes out the door carrying child #3 in order to corral child #1 and child #2, while you whip off #4's diaper, slap on a clean one, redo the diaper tabs and strap her back into the carrier. You reach the van just in time to hear child #2 say, "Mommy, I have to go potty."

When you get to the restaurant, you still have to get all your children into the building. You open the rear passenger door of the van and stand there as the two older ones pile out and your husband unbuckles the two younger ones. When all the kids are unbuckled and out of the van, your husband starts for the door, and the kids follow behind him like ducklings, with you bringing up the rear. The kids head right inside while your husband holds the door open, and you try to squeeze past them so they don't run rampant once they reach the seating area. Once you're all standing in a little group, the hostess approaches you, carrying some menus. She leads you to a table at the back of the restaurant, past millions of other diners, all of whom your kids have to stop and stare at.

Finally, you're there, and you manage to get everyone seated. The hostess hands you the menus and escapes. Your waitress shows up a few minutes later, while you're in the midst of putting the little jelly tubs on a neighboring table so the kids won't eat any more of them. She says, "Wow, you guys sure have your hands full."

"It's kind of like juggling monkeys," your husband says.

Sounds about right, doesn't it? The main difference being that monkeys can strap themselves into their high chairs.

When you're pregnant, you don't think about the fact that in a way, pregnancy is the easy part. At least when you're pregnant, your baby is easily contained. She's not going to escape and run into the parking lot. He's not going to be busy eating the condiments while you're not looking because you're picking up his sister's pacifier from the floor. Baby's staying right where it's easy to keep an eye on her . . . until Birth Day comes.

That's when things get difficult to manage. Do you clean while the baby's sleeping, or do you use that time to rest? Should you leave now and interfere with naptime, or wait until later and miss supper? Or the ultimate—how can you get more than one child to smile at the camera at the same time, everyone with his or her eyes open and nobody's finger in his or her nose?

Raising children is difficult. Whether you have one child or more than one, things can and will get crazy. There are times when you'll wonder how you're ever going to manage everything that needs to get done, and there's just no way around that.

I used to think that if I were sufficiently organized, I'd be able to keep everyone happy and everything clean at the same time. Um . . . no. It doesn't work that way. You and I, hard as we might try, are not capable of managing everything with no messes or slip-ups.

Aren't you glad that God is able to do a perfect job in managing His children? I sure am. I am glad that He doesn't have trouble managing more than one child at the same time. He can always give each of us the individual parenting we need without becoming exhausted or depleted. And He's never too busy helping someone else to pay attention to my needs. He can handle all of us at the same time.

So the next time you're trying to juggle monkeys, let the occasion remind you to praise God for His infinite ability to deal well with all His children.

And if you need any juggling lessons, just ask Him. He's a willing Teacher.

I am the LORD, the God of all mankind. Is anything too hard for me?
JEREMIAH 32:27

REFLECTION QUESTIONS

1. Isn't it amazing how God can lovingly rear all of His children at the same time?

2. Is it hard for you to manage your child(ren), logistically speaking? Is there someone you could ask for help in making things run a little easier?

6

More than Enough

I love it when my children ask me to play with them. Knowing they're choosing to be with me because they want to, not just because they have to, makes me feel loved and needed. Even if I'm right in the middle of doing something else when they ask, I try to make time for them as soon as I can. I'm well aware that all too soon they'll want to play more with their friends than with me, and their sweet requests for time together will be mostly memories.

One day, as I sat at the computer working, Jessica walked in from the playroom. She was carrying a random assortment of play food, plates, and utensils clutched in her little arms. "Please play with me," she asked.

My heart melted. I pushed the keyboard tray back into its home and sat down on the floor with her. Jessica divided the items, with each of us getting a utensil or two and some kind of food. She put a hot dog bun on my plate and sat down with her spoon, cup, and box of cereal.

We played contentedly for a while, tasting our food. "Thank you for this delicious food," I said.

"You're welcome," Jessica replied sweetly.

Jessica didn't seem to notice that she had brought insufficient food for a "real" meal, or that a real meal with these particular foods would have been a strange one, indeed. As far as she was concerned, we each had something to eat and something to eat it with, and that was all we needed.

Have you noticed how kids can be content with nearly nothing? Sure, they often request $300 items for their birthday, because they don't yet understand the difference between $300 and $3. But all my kids' best toys seem to have cost a dollar or been bought at a garage sale (or to have been the box an expensive toy came in). Somehow, they find more delight in these items than in the more costly things I sometimes buy them. And did you know that the cardboard box is the only non-toy item to have been officially inducted into the Toy Hall of Fame?

We need to take a lesson from our children and learn to be content with what God has given us. Far too often, we focus on the things we don't have, rather than the many things we do. We fail to be satisfied with the material blessings God's provided, because we think there are certain other things we need before we can "play." We have to have everything, and have it "just so," before we can be content.

Often, we fail to see the immense potential in the things around us. We look at a cardboard box and see something that needs to be taken to the curb for trash pick-up, instead of the makings of a spaceship, a grocery store, or a cave. We survey our children's toys and see the lack of toys we wish they had instead of realizing, hey, they have a bucket, a shovel, and some dirt, so they don't really need anything else. Our old, beat-up muffin tin doesn't remind us of all the memories we've made along with the muffins; instead, it makes us wish for a new one.

Our kids take their satisfaction cues from us. If they hear us regularly complain about our house, our car, or our entertainment system, they'll learn to complain about their possessions, too. When they see us buying things we can't afford, they'll discount the blessings of what they have and always wish for more.

I'm not suggesting that material things are bad in themselves. Many, if not most, of them are morally neutral. But even good things become a snare to us when our focus on obtaining them prevents us from being content with what God has already provided.

God gives us what He has determined is sufficient for us. When we consistently fail to be content with the amount of His provision, it's like telling Him that He hasn't done enough. Most of us would never say those words out loud, but our actions clearly show that we believe them to be true. Sometimes, we even resent people who have more than we do, because we think we should have those things too.

Oh, if only we could truly absorb into our hearts and lives what the Bible teaches—that if we have food and clothing, we should be content with that.

When Jessica and I played that day, we had plenty of fun. Our fun wouldn't have been any greater if we'd had a complete set of china and a grocery store at our disposal.

Sometimes, a hot dog, a spoon, and a box of cereal are more than enough.

> *Keep your lives free from the love of money and*
> *be content with what you have, because God has said,*
> *"Never will I leave you; never will I forsake you."*
> HEBREWS 13:5

REFLECTION QUESTIONS

1. Is there something in your home that you don't appreciate? What further possibilities can you see in it?

2. Are you content with what God has given you, or do you often need more? If your answer is "more," how can you learn to be more content with what you have?

7

The Ten Commandments, Revised

I bet when Moses brought the Ten Commandments down from the mountain, he never realized how many interesting discussions they would generate among people who wouldn't be born yet for thousands of years. Around our house, for instance, the Commandments have caused all kinds of issues to arise before I expected them.

For example, one day when the kids and I were driving home from Walmart, Ellie asked, out of the blue, "What is 'adultery'?" She was five at the time. I had thought it would be several years yet before that subject came up. I mean, Ellie didn't (and still doesn't!) even know what S-E-X is, so how in the world would I explain adultery?

Thinking quickly, I said, "Um, it's acting like you're married to somebody when you're not."

Whew, thank You, God. That was a close one, I prayed, figuring I had narrowly averted disaster.

"Why would anybody want to do that?" Ellie asked.

I was fresh out of creative answers. So this time, I pulled out the response that has never failed me yet. "We'll talk about that when you're older," I said.

Another time, there was a different discussion. We were actually talking about the Ten Commandments, what they were, and why God gave them to us. Ellie is my child who wants to make sure she knows exactly what she's supposed to do. "So do we have to keep *all* of them?" she asked.

"Yes, that's the idea," I said.

"Oh." She paused a few seconds. "Like, even the one about 'honor your father and mother'?"

"Yes, that one too," I said.

The funniest Ten Commandments discussion we've ever had (I know, you didn't know there *was* such a thing as a funny conversation about the Ten Commandments) happened shortly after Ellie turned six. Our entire family was sitting at the table eating lunch when Ellie announced excitedly, "I'm going to say the Ten Commandments."

I figured this would be pretty interesting, as we hadn't yet required her to memorize them, and I invited her to go ahead.

"The Father is a Son and Holy Spirit, so you can't have any other gods before Him," Ellie began. Okay, not exactly word for word, but so far, so good.

"You shall not covet," she continued. "Obey your father and your mother, or else, WHACK!"

My husband and I burst out laughing. Ellie wasn't quite sure what was so funny, but she laughed too. The other three kids joined in with our laughter because they didn't want to be left out.

Ellie had clearly absorbed the concept that if she didn't obey her dad and me, she would suffer the consequences. And as far as she knew at that point, the reason to obey was to avoid getting in trouble. What was so funny was hearing the Ten Commandments viewed through the eyes of a child.

What wasn't funny at all was realizing that often, we moms see the Commandments that way too.

Obey God . . . or else.

Isn't that how we often view the Ten Commandments? As nothing more than rules to obey so we don't get punished? They certainly are that, but they are so much more. They are God's guidelines for rendering Him proper worship and acting the way we're supposed to. What we don't often realize is that they're also guidelines that He has designed to allow us to enjoy our lives to the fullest.

God knows how life works far better than we do. He knows exactly what is necessary for us to experience life—and Him—to the fullest. In His grace, He wrote down the rules for us so that we could have them to follow. He's not some cosmic killjoy who's out to ruin our fun. He's a loving Father who wants to show us how to receive all the benefits He has in store for us.

Don't steal. Not because He doesn't want us to have material possessions, but because He wants to teach us the joy of working for them.

Remember the Sabbath, and keep it holy. Not because He's a legalist, but because He wants us to experience the joy of resting from our labors as we rest in Him.

Don't have any other gods before me. Not because He's egotistical, but because He knows that only in Him will we find our greatest fulfillment.

It makes a big difference in the strength of our desire to obey when we see the Ten Commandments as guidelines to the abundant life rather than 10 ways to restrict us.

So let's obey them. Yes, all of them. But instead of obeying because we have to, let's obey because we realize they are what is best for us. And let's thank God for laying out so clearly the road to blessing.

> *For this is the love of God, that we keep his commandments.*
> *And his commandments are not burdensome.*
> 1 JOHN 5:3, *ESV*

REFLECTION QUESTIONS

1. Do you see God's commands as restricting your fun or showing you the way to abundant life?

2. Why do you obey God? Because you have to, because you love Him, or both, depending on the situation?

8

Skilled Building

My husband and I enjoy having guests in our home. Because Phil works in the evenings, we don't get to entertain as often as we'd like. But one particular evening, he didn't have to work, so we invited another couple to come over. After dinner, we allowed the kids to run off and play while the adults remained at the table talking. Outside, a neighbor walked past the dining room windows carrying some pieces of lumber, and the conversation turned to construction and how Phil had served as the general contractor for an addition to our home.

"I'd bring in the plumbers or electricians and say, 'I want this done,' and they'd do it," my husband said. We found it amazing how workers can come in and quickly and efficiently do something that's far beyond our own capabilities. If you get enough people together who all do their jobs in this way, you wind up with an excellent product, a home that someone will be proud to live in. Each person brings his or her individual expertise, and working together, the house gets built.

The Body of Christ works the same way. God has gifted each one of us with a certain area of expertise. Some are electricians, some are plumbers, and some are painters. No one has exactly the same skills as any other person, but that's okay. When you put the entire Body together, all the skills are present that are needed to accomplish God's work.

Most of us wouldn't attempt to be the general contractor to build a home. We recognize that we don't have the knowledge and experience necessary to do an adequate job. Yet we make the momentous mistake of assuming that we *do* know how to run the Body of Christ.

Not one of us knows how to run the Body by herself. Why? Put simply, we're not God. He's the only one qualified to be the general contractor, for many reasons. Not the least is the fact that only He knows exactly what the finished product should look like. Another important reason is that He's God—and we're not. In Him resides all authority for designing the home and choosing the laborers. In Him rests the ability to dispense to those laborers, as He sees fit, the ability to do their jobs.

When we were building the addition to our home, the various subcontractors came to the house at all hours of the day and sometimes on weekends. I usually knew what they were there to do, but I didn't understand why they did it the way they did, or why my husband chose to have some workers come before others. But this lack of knowledge didn't compel me to interrupt their work, throw them out, and try to finish the job myself. Instead, it made me realize that I would have to put my trust in my husband to know what he was doing, or the job would not be finished properly.

Likewise, even when we don't understand why God is going about things in a certain way, we shouldn't interfere. He knows why all the workers are necessary. He chose these workers—and not others—for a particular reason. He knows what the finished product will look like, and when it will be completed. So let's not imagine that we know better than He does, and that we could get the house built better or sooner. Let's let Him be about His business.

Our job is not to make the decisions but to work under His direction in order to carry out His decisions. If we're busy trying to do a job we weren't meant to do, we run the risk of either messing up the job or missing out on the blessings of doing what we should have been doing.

So let's not rely on our own wisdom to supervise the building. Let's each do our part, under the direction of the Holy Spirit, and *He* will make sure Christ's house is built excellently.

*The whole body depends on Christ, and all the parts of the
body are joined and held together. Each part does its own work
to make the whole body grow and be strong with love.*
EPHESIANS 4:16, *NCV*

REFLECTION QUESTIONS

1. What gifts has God given you to be used for the benefit of the Body of Christ?

2. How are you currently using your gifts to serve the
   Body?

9

Foreverrrrrr

"Mommy, how much longer?" Kenny begged, looking up at me beseechingly with his big brown eyes. He stood poised and ready to head out the door as soon as I gave the word.

I had promised to take the kids to the park. But there were some things I needed to put in order around the house before we went. Kenny had checked every two or three minutes to see if it was time yet. Now his patience was wearing thin.

"Son, it's still going to be awhile yet," I said.

"But how many *minutes*?"

"Ten minutes," I guessed.

Kenny collapsed to the floor. "But that'll take *forever!*"

"I know it seems like forever," I said, in what I hoped was my "patient" voice.

Kenny sighed and slumped forward. He propped his elbows on the floor and plunked his chin into his cupped hands. It was obvious from his posture and the frown on his face that "soon" wasn't soon enough.

I completely identified with what Kenny was feeling. I'm not a very patient person either. I'm action-oriented. I much prefer doing something to waiting around for something to happen. I actually prayed for patience once; boy, did God send me a lot of opportunities to work on developing it. But I still have a long way to go in this area.

Over the years, I've learned to control the outward expressions of my impatience—most of the time, at least. I've learned to take deep breaths, remind myself that "this, too, shall pass," and all the other things a person is supposed to do. But inwardly, my heart still has trouble waiting.

I find it especially difficult to wait in two particular kinds of situations: when I'm grieving, and when I'm longing for a desire to be fulfilled.

Obviously, no one likes to grieve. No one wants to suffer or experience pain you can't do much about. When you're grieving, minutes can take hours. Waiting for hope and healing to come seems like it truly does take *forever*, and even then, it comes only in stages. If only there were a definite end to the hurt, we think we might be able to make it through the waiting. But life doesn't work that way.

Longing for something and not seeing our desire fulfilled can be hard. The Bible says that hope deferred makes the heart sick (see Prov. 13:12). I've certainly felt that way at times. I've wondered if what I longed for was *ever* going to come to pass. And it hasn't been easy to wait, especially when the results have mattered *so much*.

But God's perception of time is not like ours. We dwell in linear time, but He's not bound by 24 hours in a day. To Him, waiting 30 minutes, or even 30 *years*, isn't forever. He doesn't consider our time waiting as time spent in limbo. Rather, He knows that through our waiting, He is accomplishing His purpose in our lives, even when it seems to us like nothing's going on. Plus, He has a completely eternal perspective, which means He sees anything we pass through in this lifetime as a stepping-stone on the way to eternal glory.

So when the dishes seem endless, when potty training looks like it will take the rest of our lives, or when making peace in a difficult relationship is taking far too long, we can find comfort in the fact that these things will *not* last forever. Even when it seems like "forever" is camping out on our doorstep, it's not so. Nothing on this earth is more than transitory.

We tend to forget that this life is not all there is. Instead, we focus on what's happening *now*, as if our circumstances are far more important than they really are. We fail to realize that our problems, challenges, and periods of waiting are mere speed bumps on the road to what awaits us.

What a difference it would make in our lives if we were to realize that each moment—even those spent waiting—brings us one moment closer to an incredibly blissful eternity, where every longing we've ever had will be fulfilled. True, some desires may go unmet on this earth, but one day, they will be met beyond measure.

And *that's* what will last forever—a glorious eternity of infinite delight.

> *For our light and momentary troubles are achieving*
> *for us an eternal glory that far outweighs them all.*
> 2 CORINTHIANS 4:17

REFLECTION QUESTIONS

1. Do you view your circumstances as the whole point of life, or as stepping-stones on the way to eternity? Either way, what difference does it make in the way you view your life?

2. How would seeing painful circumstances as fleeting and temporary change the way you endure them?

10

No Laughing Matter

Shortly after Jessica turned two, she went through a stage where she really didn't like having her diaper changed. I mean, she *really* didn't like it. When I laid her down to change her, she acted like I was killing her. "No! No!" she would shout, kicking and thrashing about like an octopus.

One particular day, she was lying on the floor while I attempted to change her diaper. "No!" she kept saying in a really pouty voice. I stayed silent and kept working, figuring that at least it was better than her screaming. But when Jessica got no reaction from me, she got more dramatic. "No!" she said louder and more forcefully, her forehead furrowing and her little lips drawing together into a pout that stuck out far enough that the proverbial horse could have sat on it.

Something about her very calculated expression struck me as funny. I turned away quickly so she wouldn't see me smile, but I was too late. Jessica has eagle eyes, and she had seen me. "No!" she commanded, now both pouty and angry.

I couldn't help it. I burst out laughing.

Of course that made her really mad, and she stopped pouting and began crying in earnest at the indignity of it all. It took me a little while to stop laughing. I was thinking about how utterly silly it was for Jessica to try to act so big and bad and in control, when I knew that she wasn't.

The thing that finally stopped my laughter was realizing that God probably feels the same way about us sometimes. Not that He laughs, because sin is never laughable. But I'll bet He looks down from heaven and sees us making plans without consulting Him, or acting as if we're in control and our wishes are supreme, and He shakes His head at us. He knows how arrogantly ridiculous it is for us to be so impressed with ourselves that we fail to submit to His instruction.

Consider the example of Satan's arrogance. Satan's name used to be Lucifer. He was the most beautiful and glorious of all God's angels. But one day, He rose up in rebellion against God with a third of the other angels. What did God do? He sure didn't take Lucifer's defiant attitude lightly. In fact, He took it so seriously that He cast Lucifer, now named Satan, and his followers out of heaven . . . out of His presence. And one day Satan and his followers will be permanently cast into eternal punishment (see Rev. 20).

Or what about Moses? Moses was the only person in the Bible ever recorded as having seen God face to face. Moses loved God, and God loved him. But one day, after putting up with yet more of the Israelites' complaining, Moses got frustrated and decided to do things his own way instead of God's way. He put himself in the place of God by acting as though his way could be easily and equally substituted for God's instructions. What happened? Moses earned the consequences of not being able to enter the Promised Land because he'd dishonored God before all the people.

There are many other examples—too many to list here. But suffice it to say that if God was not pleased when the ancients opposed Him, He won't be pleased when we do it, either.

Most of us wouldn't openly defy God, as Jessica defied me. We wouldn't be willing to look Him in the face and say, "No. I won't follow You." Our rebellion manifests itself in other ways. We don't pray or read our Bibles regularly because we're "too busy." We don't witness to someone God points out to us because we're afraid or we don't want to get rejected. We're unwilling to speak a word of truth to someone because we don't want to offend.

I never used to think of those things as rebellion. But if we define rebellion as refusing to submit to or fulfill someone's lawful commands, then by behaving in that way, we are setting ourselves in opposition to God's commands and authority.

Yikes. That means that I've been as rebellious before God as two-year-old Jessica was that day lying on the floor. Oh, my rebellion doesn't look the same, but it is rebellion nonetheless.

Our rebellion can take many different forms. All are equally sinful and equally damaging to our relationship with God. When we rebel, we try to stretch the relationship into something it was never meant to be—a relationship between a superior and a subordinate, but with ourselves in the superior position.

Instead of trying to take the place of God, let's accept the place He's already given us, as His dearly beloved children. As the old song says, let's "[do] exactly what the Lord commands, doing it happily." For His commands are not burdensome. They are the pathway to the abundant life of glorifying God and enjoying Him forever.

> *Moreover, we have all had human fathers who disciplined us*
> *and we respected them for it. How much more should we*
> *submit to the Father of our spirits and live!*
>
> HEBREWS 12:9

REFLECTION QUESTIONS

1. Which of God's commands do you tend to have difficulty following (or refuse to follow)? Why?

2. How can you submit your heart more fully to God in these areas?

11

Facing Life's Tangles

My oldest daughter used to have really curly hair. I say *used to* because as she grew older, Ellie's hair got straighter and straighter, until it's only slightly wavy now. But it still gets tangled pretty easily, especially underneath at the back of her head. To make matters worse, she's tender-headed. Any time I have to comb her hair, it's a really unpleasant experience for both of us.

I pointed out to her that if she would learn to do her own hair, I wouldn't have to do it, and it might not hurt as much. Ellie was willing to try just about anything, so she got out the brush and began to try to draw it through her hair.

But I could tell from the sound of the brush on her hair that she wasn't getting all the way through it. "Let me help you," I suggested.

"No, I'll do it," she said.

"You're not getting all the tangles out," I said.

Ellie ran the brush through her hair one more time. She sighed and complained, "Every time I do my hair, I find more tangles."

"That's because you skim over the surface when you do it," I said. "You don't get all the way down to the tangles."

Just skimming the surface . . . we moms do that too, don't we? We want a problem resolved, so we give it a good swipe and pronounce it taken care of. The only problem is, we haven't gotten down to the nitty-gritty. So it crops up again later, and we're bewildered that it's back. We frown and mentally say, *I thought I already took care of that.* But we never really got down to the root of the problem.

It's kind of like cleaning the house before company comes when you don't really have time to get the job done right. You start taking shortcuts, because you have to. In our house, this takes the form of piling everything there's no time for in the master bedroom and shutting the door. The house looks clean when our company arrives. But when it's time to go to bed, the mess is right there. It hasn't disappeared. It's just been moved around a bit.

That's what happens when we try to work out a problematic issue without really letting God have our heart about it. We may try to smooth things over in a difficult relationship without going before God so that He can show us our part in the difficulties and grant us a supernatural love for the other person. Or worse yet, we try to maintain our relationship with Him by doing all the right things, such as Bible study, church attendance and prayer, yet we temporarily forget that it's not about doing; it's about *being*. So even while we're doing everything "right," we've failed to do the most important thing of all—lay our heart before God and let Him change it.

Christianity is supposed to be about an intimate relationship with Jesus, not how many "Christian-y" things we do. Don't get me wrong; many of these things are vitally important parts of our spiritual life. But they are means to an end, not the end in themselves.

If we want to draw closer to God (and if we don't, that's a whole other problem), we need to focus on the first and greatest commandment, and the second that is like unto it: we should seek to love God with everything we are, and to love our neighbor as ourselves. Increased Bible study and worship service attendance may be a part of how we do this. But when we focus on the actions instead of on the commandments, we're not getting down to the tangles. It's like making the surface of our hair look nice, when underneath, there's still a mess.

It takes courage to get down to the tangles. I'm sure Ellie would agree. But in order for her hair to be completely taken care of, we have to do it.

Are we moms willing to courageously get down to the tangles in our own lives? Whether those snarled areas represent issues that have never been resolved or matters we've just never paid attention to, they're still there, even if we can't see them beneath the carefully arranged beauty on the surface.

It's hard to face the tangles. And yes, it might hurt. But if we want our lives to be truly tangle-free, we have to work on them. We have to get down to business. When the grooming's done, we'll be tangle-free, and the pain will have been worth it.

Surely you desire truth in the inner parts.
You teach me wisdom in the inmost place.
PSALM 51:6

REFLECTION QUESTIONS

1. Are there tangles in your life that are hard to deal with? Are there areas of pain you'd prefer to keep hidden? What do these questions bring to mind?

2. Are you ready to share those secret places with God (and perhaps another trusted person) and let Him help you work through these areas? If not, what would have to happen before you were ready?

12

No Getting Away with It

Ellie has a strong sense of right and wrong. She knows our family rules well enough to know that when someone violates them, there should be consequences—unless special circumstances warrant an exception.

Apparently, she didn't think leniency was justified one day when she came running into the bathroom as I stood at the bathroom counter brushing my hair. "Mommy!" she reported. "Kenny's just sitting on the floor trying to build something with his K'Nex. He's not cleaning up."

I had told all the kids to work on getting their rooms clean. We do this every day (and sometimes multiple times a day), so the kids know how to straighten up. But on this day, Kenny was apparently having more fun creating some kind of structure than creating cleanliness.

"You're not cleaning up, either," I pointed out. "You're in here."

"Aren't you even going to punish somebody who's disobeying?" Ellie asked incredulously, trying to make my actions—or lack thereof—make sense.

I can see her point. After all, she came by her black-and-white perspective from me. One of my directives had indeed been broken, and Ellie was advising me of that fact so that I could do the "right" thing—which in this case, she was sure, was to administer consequences to her brother.

She was right. But she was wrong in assuming that just because I didn't immediately go talk to Kenny, he wasn't going to receive any consequences. All she saw was that I wasn't doing what she expected me to do when she expected me to do it, so she concluded that I wasn't going to do anything, ever.

Just like Ellie, most of us moms have an innate sense of what's right and wrong and how justice should be administered in the world. When other people—not ourselves, mind you, but others—sin and seemingly get away with it, we resent it. We get stopped for speeding and receive a ticket, and it makes us mad that "everybody else" can speed on their merry way and "never" have to pay for their sin. Or we know people who lie, and it seems to bring them an advantage over their circumstances. I know there've been times when I've resented having to "walk the straight and narrow" while others got to do anything they wanted.

That attitude is deeply, seriously wrong, and there are at least two reasons why. First, sinning may bring us more earthly advantages and may even seem to bring us more fun, but it is ultimately nowhere near as satisfying to our souls as walking in right relationship with God. If we think we'd have more fun if we had fewer constraints, we've bought into Satan's lie that God's ways are dull, while sin brings life. We couldn't be more mistaken.

The second reason is that even though we think people might be getting away with things, no one is really getting away with anything. At the Judgment, sinners will be forced to admit they made wrong choices and deserve only hell as their consequences. And hell is exactly what they'll get. Christians, on the other hand, won't go to hell, but we'll still have to give an account of our every word and act. And then we'll realize, as we have never realized before, that our sins cost Jesus His life. Jesus paid for the things we didn't have to pay for.

God is completely righteous, just and holy, and He will not sweep anybody's sin under the rug. Someone has to pay for it. Either we'll pay for it ourselves, or Jesus will pay for us and we'll spend forever with Him in heaven, glorifying Him for His great goodness and willingness to save us from ourselves.

So the next time we're tempted to think that somebody is getting away with something, let's remind ourselves that nobody ever gets away with anything. Let's trust God to assess consequences in His own time frame and not worry about being the ones to try to make sure it happens. After all, we have enough to worry about if we're serious about dealing with the sin in our own lives. Or at least, I do. Maybe you do too.

What shall we say, then? Shall we go on sinning so that grace may increase? By no means! We died to sin; how can we live in it any longer?

ROMANS 6:1-2

Through Christ Jesus the law of the Spirit of life set me free from the law of sin and death.

ROMANS 8:2

REFLECTION QUESTIONS

1. Do you ever resent someone's "getting away with something" while you have to do the right thing? What is your inner conversation like?

2. Have you bought into Satan's lie that sin brings life while God's law brings death? If so, what do you need to do to adjust your perspective?

13

Roly-Poly Summer

Someday when I'm old, and I think back on life when the kids were small, I will always remember this summer as the Summer of the Roly-Polies.

I don't remember how my son, Kenny, first became interested in roly-polies. I think it all started when my husband began digging up dirt for a small garden he intended to plant in our backyard. Of course, if dirt is involved, Kenny is right there in the midst of the project, and this time was no exception.

My husband spent hours in the backyard digging up our hard-packed lawn, turning over the soil and mixing it with whatever gardeners mix soil with (you can tell how much I know about gardening). Kenny was right there with him, helping dig, or just watching his progress. When my husband dug down deep enough to reach the dirt that wasn't so hard-packed, and then when he began turning it over, some beautiful, glorious, rich black earth was revealed. And among the clods were . . . roly-polies! Lots and lots of them.

It turns out roly-polies love rich, moist soil, so they were doing their best to burrow back into it. Kenny, on the other hand, was doing his utmost to catch them. He would reach down with thumb and forefinger and actually *touch* them, squeezing them just enough to lift them up and collect them in a plastic container I had formerly used for leftover food. Several times over the next few days, he invited me to go out and look for roly-polies with him, and I obliged whenever I could. There's just something wholesome and heartwarming about helping your son catch bugs. (Although I must say, I will only go so far. Roly-polies are on my "tolerable" list; most other bugs are not.)

When my husband finished planting the garden, and Kenny was no longer allowed to root through the dirt looking for roly-polies (lest he disturb the seeds), he took his roly-poly hunting to the front yard. We have bushes in front of our home, with a border and some mulch making them into nice-looking beds. Kenny discovered that roly-polies loved our front yard, too, and every morning, he faithfully went outside to collect some.

We had to explain to him at one point that when they're lying on their backs all still like that, they're dead, and maybe you should put a little water in the box next time; but for the most part, the hunting and maintenance went without a hitch. One time, Kenny even decided to release his considerable collection back into the wild again (that is, underneath our bushes) so he could re-catch them the next day.

Kenny loves looking for those little creatures. He is absolutely dedicated to finding them. His best delight is when he spots a group of them and can seize several at once. Then he brings them to me in a grubby clenched fist, and says, "Wanna see how many roly-polies I got?" He opens his hand to reveal 10 or 12, or sometimes more, squiggly brown bugs squirming all over each other in the dirt-encrusted creases of his hand.

The point is that Kenny was—and still is—enjoying the stuffing out of God's creation. He's delighting in it. He's discovering things God has made and considering them marvelous.

When was the last time you and I took time to really appreciate God's creation? I'm not suggesting our appreciation should necessarily come in the form of a handful of creepy-crawlies. But it should definitely come in some form.

What do you appreciate about God's creation? I don't mean just what do you think is kind of neat, but what do you really love about it? Can't think of anything? Neither could I when I first asked myself this question. I mean, sure, I like rainbows and trees and flowers, but I don't have the same level of admiration for them that Kenny seems to have for his roly-polies. I don't get terribly excited about finding a rainbow or a flower. At most, I usually say to myself, *Oh, that's neat.* At the least, I don't even notice them.

I bet God enjoys Kenny's attitude toward His creation a lot more than He enjoys mine. I bet He just loves it when someone really, I mean, *really* appreciates what He's created, instead of taking it mostly for granted. After all, He's given us a world full of things to enjoy, so I'm pretty sure He means for us to spend time enjoying them.

As I think more about what part of God's creation I most appreciate, I realize that I love rain. I really do. I love that smell in the air; I love how it makes the sky overcast, which seems to make the world more peaceful; and I love dancing in the rain. That's the kind of enjoyment I think God intends for us to get from His creation.

The next time it rains, if you are driving along and see a woman out dancing in her front yard, well, you know who it'll be. Come join me, and we'll enjoy God's world together.

> *For you make me glad by your deeds, O Lord;*
> *I sing for joy at the works of your hands.*
> PSALM 92:4

REFLECTION QUESTIONS

1. Which aspects of God's creation do you truly delight in?

2. How can you spend time enjoying at least one of those aspects this week?

14

Why Not?

I just witnessed a small child wearing two headbands—one pink, one blue denim rhinestone-studded—a purple T-shirt, a diaper (no shorts), and orange fairy wings, trying to put pink fuzzy slippers with multicolored polka dots into my refrigerator. No, really. And no, I didn't have anything stronger than 1% milk with my breakfast this morning.

Jessica looked up at me as I came to a stop beside the fridge. I stared at her, trying to think of something to say. I opted for verifying what I was seeing. "Jessica, are you putting your *slippers* into the *refrigerator*?" I asked.

"Mm-hmm," she said, grinning.

I tried to think of a reason why she might be doing this. The best reason I could come up with was, *Why not?* So I said, "Slippers don't go in the refrigerator, silly," and Jessica laughed as if she'd just played the practical joke of the century.

She's not the only one of my kids who likes to do interesting things I never would have thought of. Once, my husband found three-year-old Lindsey rifling through a box of gallon-size freezer bags he'd left sitting on the counter. "What are you doing?" he asked, knowing that if he didn't intervene, there might very well be freezer bags scattered all over the house pretty soon.

Lindsey grasped one of the bags tightly in her small fist. She looked up at him and said, "I'm going to go find things and put them in the bag and collect them."

"What kinds of things?" he asked.

"Butterflies, bees and pennies," she said.

He let her have the bag.

Kids don't think the same way we do. (But then, if you're a mom, you already knew that.) For one thing, they only see possibilities, not limitations. If you ask my five-year-old son, Kenny, who's the strongest, fastest, most intelligent boy in the world, he'll tell you that he is. He's not being arrogant; he just really appreciates what his body can do. Or ask four-year-old Lindsey whether she's a fast runner, and she'll say, "*Vewy* fast." Neither of them has yet learned the adult skill of comparing ourselves to others and finding that one's own skills come up short. As far as they know at this point in their lives, they might really be the "-est." Even when they were confronted with irrefutable evidence that other kids are faster (such as when they ran in a Kiddie K last year), they still appreciate their own abilities. They haven't yet reached the stage where they don't appreciate what *they* can do just because others do it better or faster. Their way of thinking isn't as "mature" as ours. But it's a lot more satisfying to them than ours is to us.

Another way kids think differently is that their minds work outside of "the way things are supposed to go" lines. Remember the slippers in the fridge? Seemed like a fun thing to do as far as Jessica was concerned. So she decided to try it and see if it was, in fact, fun. Oh, I know she didn't think of it that way in her little mind. But she expected it to be enjoyable, so she did it. She didn't think to herself, as we often do, *Well, that's a new thing. I better not try it, because I might not be able to do it. And even if I could, I probably wouldn't enjoy it.*

Why do we stop thinking like kids? Okay, granted, there are some areas and situations where we wouldn't want to think like a two-year-old. If you and I are standing in line at the grocery store, and you bump into me, I shouldn't push you back—or worse yet, bite you. So yeah, we do need to mature. But there are some ways in which we need to remain like little children.

First, we need to appreciate the abilities God has given us. Just because you're a better cook than I am doesn't mean I should feel bad about myself or my cooking skills. And if I'm a better racquetball player than you, that doesn't mean you should decide you're never going to pick up a piece of competitive sporting equipment again. God made me to play racquetball. He made you to cook. So instead of feeling bad that we're not the "-est" in some area, we should just be glad we are what we are. That's not to say we can never improve. But it does mean we should be satisfied with the basic abilities God gave us and not wish we were just like somebody else.

Second, when we look at something we've never tried before, we should see the possibilities of everything that could go right instead of everything that could go wrong. True, we might not be very good at the new activity. But so what? If it's not sinful, and if we have fun doing it, then what does it matter if we're not the Olympic champion at it? If we only stick to tried-and-true things, we'll fail to discover all kinds of fun. We'll miss out on a million things we could have enjoyed if we had only seen the possibilities and tried them out.

So the next time your child does something that leaves you shaking your head and thinking, *Huh?*, stop a minute. Think about whether you might not be able to use a little inventiveness in your own life.

You probably shouldn't store your polka-dot slippers in the fridge, but maybe you'll find something else to do that's even better.

Now the Lord is the Spirit, and where the Spirit of the Lord is, there is freedom.
2 CORINTHIANS 3:17, *ESV*

REFLECTION QUESTIONS

1. Do you like to try new things? Why or why not?

2. Is there something new you'd like to try, but you've been hesitating? Why not make plans to pursue it?

15

Train Fright

I take my kids outside to play as often as I can. That's because I think running around outdoors is good for them in a number of ways. They have more space in which to play, they can feel the sun on their faces and the wind in their hair, and they even get to dig in the dirt, right there in the midst of God's amazing world. They sleep better at night, too. So whenever it's not too blazing hot, we spend as much time outside as we can.

A couple of years ago, I had all four kids outside with me. Jessica, still an infant, was sitting on the porch with me. Ellie, Kenny, and Lindsey played at various pursuits in the yard. The weather was nice, and everything was going along just fine until I heard . . . the dreaded sound.

Woo-woooooooo! Woo-woooooooo!

The train was still quite a ways away, but its whistle could easily be heard as it approached. Lindsey's head came up from looking at whatever she was playing with. Before the sound had died away, she was running headlong, screaming, from the other side of the yard, toward me where I sat on the porch.

The rumble of the train's immense bulk chugging over the rails got louder, and the whistle sounded again as Lindsey charged up the steps and flung herself into my arms. She wrapped her arms and legs around me and clung to me as tightly as she could. I hugged her close and held her securely until the train had passed by and the air was quiet. She was ready to get up then, and I released her so she could go back to her play.

Lindsey didn't know that she didn't have to be scared of the train. Her fear was instinctive, and even though it wasn't necessary, it was very real to her. Though she had the wrong idea about what she should fear, she had the right idea about what to do when she was scared. She fled immediately to the arms of the one who could keep her safe.

We should do the same thing when we're afraid. We should run unhesitatingly to the embrace of the one who can keep us secure.

God loves us, far more even than I loved Lindsey that day she ran to the shelter of my arms. Because He loves us more than we can imagine, He has made Himself available whenever we need to come to Him. And even better than sitting on the porch, where we can get to Him if we need to, He has placed His Spirit within us, so that we're always in the presence of God. It takes even less time for us to come into God's presence than it did for Lindsey to run across our yard as fast as her legs would take her.

What an incredible gift! God Himself is ready and willing to comfort us whenever we bring our fears to Him. He'll wrap His arms around us and hold us close in His lap until our fear subsides and we're ready to get back on our feet.

And He won't belittle our fears. Just as I would never have dreamed of telling Lindsey that her fears were ridiculous and making her feel ashamed for feeling that way, so too God will not disparage our feelings. He may correct us, showing us a better or more righteous way to feel. But He won't shame us for being human.

After all, God made us this way, and He knows that emotions are a part of being a finite human with limited understanding. There will be times when our emotions do not please Him, and He will lovingly correct us at those times. But He won't mock us. He won't humiliate us. He'll treat us tenderly, even when He has to correct us firmly.

We should rejoice in the fact that we can bring every emotion we have to Him—fear, anger, joy, sorrow, anything at all—and still find His arms open to receive us. Nothing we feel will surprise Him. None of our emotions will cause Him to think less of us or love us any less. Unrighteous emotions will offend Him, but only because He knows they are neither for His glory nor for our benefit. And even then, His goal in helping us handle our emotions will be to restore us to a closer relationship with Himself.

What an amazingly loving God! What a wonderful, compassionate Father! Why would we ever hesitate to come to Him?

The Lord is my rock and my fortress and my deliverer,
my God, my rock, in whom I take refuge, my shield,
and the horn of my salvation, my stronghold.
PSALM 18:2, *ESV*

REFLECTION QUESTIONS

1. When trouble comes, do you flee to your Father? If not, why not?

2. When you flee to God in your times of trouble, what do you receive from Him? If you flee to other "comforts," how do they compare?

16

You Made Me Do It!

Some time ago, my husband and I realized that though we served vegetables with each meal, the kids almost never ate them. We nagged and cajoled them to eat more vegetables, but it seemed they were always too full to do so. So my husband came up with a plan: We'd tell them they had to eat their vegetables first, before they got anything else that was on the table. If they didn't eat some vegetables, they wouldn't be able to move on to the entrée, and they would therefore get no bedtime snack. We crossed our fingers and implemented the plan.

What do you know, it worked! Suddenly, when our kids were faced with the prospect of not getting pizza until they ate their green beans, eating vegetables became tolerable. Our only exception to this rule is that each child may choose one fruit or vegetable that he or she doesn't want to eat. Whenever I serve the item they dislike, they may skip it and have the entrée only.

Such was the case one evening when my husband was at work and the kids and I were sitting at the table having dinner. Ellie had passed on the applesauce, because she hates it. Turkey was the main course that night, and she didn't eat much of it either. "I want to be done," she said.

"Okay," I said, "but that means you won't get a snack." Anticipating her motive for wanting to be done so quickly, I added, "And you can't just leave the table and go play computer games."

"I wasn't thinking about that until you 'idea-ed' me," Ellie said.

"Sorry," I replied.

"I wouldn't have been like that if you hadn't made me think about it," Ellie continued.

I wonder if Eve thought the same way in the Garden of Eden. "I wouldn't have been so interested in that one tree if God hadn't told me I couldn't eat it." I don't know whether or not she ever thought that, but I do know that she blamed her sin on somebody else.

We're the same way. We blame our sins on others for "giving us the idea." After all, if they hadn't provoked us by tempting us, we never would have thought of sinning in that way. Or if we had thought of it, at least we would have been able to resist if they hadn't stirred us up.

The Bible clearly teaches that we are each responsible for our own sin. Yes, the devil, other people, or circumstances may tempt us, but we are the ones responsible for choosing whether or not to succumb to temptation. If we do, it's nobody's fault but our own.

If you have more than one child, I bet there have been times when one child has blamed the other for his or her actions. We struggle with this issue in our household. When one child gets called to account, he or she wants to say, "Well, but my sister/brother did such-and-such." They want to share the blame or at least mitigate their own failure.

What we're trying to teach them to do is take responsibility for their sin. When I ask a child if he or she did something, I want the child to look straight at me and say, "Yes, ma'am" or "No, ma'am." I don't want to hear what a sibling did. I want the child to own up to his or her failing.

That's what God wanted in the Garden of Eden, too. He knew very well who had done what, yet He came to the garden and posed a question, offering Adam and Eve the chance to come clean. In response, Eve said, "Well, You can't really blame me, because the serpent talked me into it." And Adam said, "God, it was the woman *You gave me* who made me do it." I wonder how their punishments might have been different if they had confessed instead of shifting the blame.

Lest we be too hard on Adam and Eve, let's remember that you and I often do the same thing. "My kids made us run late, so I had to speed to get where we were going on time, and I got a ticket, but I really didn't deserve it." Or, "Well, I didn't want to hurt her feelings, so I lied."

Mom, it's no one's fault but our own if we sin. We can't blame it on our husband, our kids, our friends, or even strangers. You and I are the ones who are in control of our actions. So when we sin, let's do the same thing we want our kids to do, because it's what God wants us to do, too. Let's admit it and accept responsibility. Then let's take it a step further and repent, because only when we're truly repentant can we be cleansed from our sin.

We can't be made clean when we're still busy blaming someone for "idea-ing" us.

When tempted, no one should say, "God is tempting me." For God cannot be tempted by evil, nor does he tempt anyone; but each one is tempted when, by his own evil desire, he is dragged away and enticed.

JAMES 1:13-14

REFLECTION QUESTIONS

1. When confronted with your sin, do you tend to make excuses? Do you feel the need to point out what others did that may have contributed to your sin?

2. If it's difficult for you to admit your sin, why is that? What needs to change in order for you to start taking responsibility for your actions?

17

Infinite Love

I'm a pretty nonviolent person. Killing bugs makes me feel bad (though it doesn't stop me from doing it). I can't go fishing because I can't stand to think the poor little fish might suffer. I don't mind if other people go fishing; I'll even eat a fish (provided that it comes in rectangular, breaded portions out of a box from the freezer section of the store). I just don't want to be the one to kill it.

I also prefer not to get involved in conflict. I'm not afraid of conflict, and I don't avoid it; I'll deal with it when it comes up. But I don't like it. I'd rather that everyone just get along.

That's why I was so surprised by something that took place shortly after my first child, Ellie, was born. It had only been a day or two since her birth, and we were still in the hospital. For the moment, as I relaxed in my bed, holding a tightly swaddled, sleeping Ellie in my arms, we were alone.

I knew that the next person through the door would probably be a nurse who had come to check on us. But suddenly, my heart was gripped by a frightening thought: *What if the next person through the door turned out not to be someone to take care of us, but to harm us? What if someone came through the door wanting to hurt my precious newborn daughter?*

My instantaneous reaction was so fierce it startled me: I would *kill* an intruder if that's what it took to defend my baby girl. And I wouldn't hesitate.

At first, I was horrified by my reaction. Where did this violent streak come from? Had it somehow lain dormant in me all the while I thought I was a peaceful person? Was it indicative of a deep-rooted sin?

The answer, of course, is no. It's the natural desire of a mother to protect her children. I know you feel the same way. Both of us would do anything necessary to keep our children safe, even to the extent of sacrificing our own lives. I've thought about it and realized that I would throw myself in front of a speeding bus if it would somehow save my child.

That's the incredible intensity of a mother's love. It goes far beyond our understanding and defies complete expression in words. And yet it is only a fraction of our heavenly Father's love for us.

A beloved hymn contains this line: "How deep the Father's love for us, how vast beyond all measure, that He should give His only Son, to make a wretch His treasure."[1] The incredible thing is not that I loved Ellie so deeply; what was truly unbelievable is that God loved me vastly more than I loved Ellie, despite the fact that I hated Him.

Oh, I never would have said I *hated* Him. But that's what a sinful nature is—being totally and completely, in one's very essence, against Him and all He stands for. Not loving Him. Not wanting Him. Yet even while my heart was a servant of the prince of this world, God loved me and sent His Son to die for me.

I didn't have to kill for Ellie, but God did kill for me.

He ordained His own Son's death on my behalf.

I wouldn't sacrifice my children for anyone in this world, and you wouldn't sacrifice yours, either. Yet that's exactly what God did. He allowed us to put His Son to death because He wanted to restore us to a love relationship with Himself. He loves us far more than we love our own precious babies that we've held in our arms.

But God didn't sacrifice Jesus just so we could have a one-time salvation experience. He intended that we should walk the rest of our lives in loving fellowship with Him. He didn't want to show us His love just once—He desires to love us every second of every day, until Jesus returns to take us all to be with Him forever.

In the midst of your day today, however it is going, He loves you and longs to be with you and share your life. You know that feeling of love that overwhelms your heart when your child snuggles close to you and says, "I love you, Mommy"? It is but a shadow of the way God feels about you *right now*. In fact, the Bible tells us that God rejoices over us with singing (see Zeph. 3:17).

Sometimes, we think our past sins prevent us from receiving God's love because we don't deserve it. In one sense, we're right. *None* of us deserves His love. But we're wrong if we think God won't love us because of something we've done. His love for us isn't based on our merit; it's based on His infinite goodness.

So the next time you hold your sleeping baby in your arms, or your preschooler climbs into your lap and just cuddles there, and your heart overflows with love, let the joy of that moment remind you of your Father's abundant love for you. Open your heart to Him, and let Him fill you with the love He longs to give you. You don't even have to know how. Just present yourself before Him, and let Him take care of the rest. He knows exactly how to minister His perfect love to your soul. And He's longing to do it if you'll just come.

The LORD your God is with you, he is mighty to save.
He will take great delight in you, he will quiet you with his love,
he will rejoice over you with singing.
ZEPHANIAH 3:17

This is love: not that we loved God, but that he loved us and
sent his Son as an atoning sacrifice for our sins.
1 JOHN 4:10

But God demonstrates his own love for us in this: While we were
still sinners, Christ died for us.
ROMANS 5:8

I pray that you, being rooted and established in love,
may have power, together with all the saints, to grasp how wide
and long and high and deep is the love of Christ, and to know
this love that surpasses knowledge—that you may be filled
to the measure of all the fullness of God.
EPHESIANS 3:17-19

REFLECTION QUESTIONS

1. Have you ever truly opened your heart to God so He can fill it with His love? If not, what holds you back?

2. Did you know that God loves you even more than you love your own children? Is that a new idea to you?

3. How can you make sure that you spend time in the next few days meditating on God's love for you?

Note

1. Stuart Townend, "How Deep the Father's Love for Us," © 1995 Kingsway's Thankyou Music.

18

Running Ahead

I've never been to a dog track or attended a dog race. But I think I know how those poor greyhounds feel chasing the rabbit. Let me explain.

At a dog track, right before the race, the race promoters release an electronic rabbit that runs along the inside rail of the track. The idea is that the dogs will chase it and run faster because they're trying to catch it. The only problem is, they'll never catch up. They'll always be several strides behind.

Sometimes, that's what it feels like in our role as a mom. Case in point: We were getting ready for a play date. It was a beautiful day, and we were preparing to meet our friends at a park my kids knew and loved. Kenny was pretty excited, and he was having a hard time waiting patiently before it was time to leave. Finally, I told him to get his shoes on, because it was almost time to go.

I was in the kitchen when I heard the front door open. I glanced in that direction and saw Kenny and Jessica heading out the door.

"Kenny, what are you doing?" I asked.

"I'm done," he said, referring to the fact that he'd finished getting ready.

"Son, I'm not quite ready yet. Please shut the door."

"Aww, man," he said, and pushed the door closed.

Sounds a lot like the way we tend to run out in front of God, doesn't it? There's somewhere we want to go, we think we're ready and we just can't wait any longer. So off we go, leaving God behind.

I bet Abraham and Sarah would have identified with Kenny, if they'd ever had the chance to meet. For just as Kenny had my promise that I would take him on a play date, the biblical couple had God's promise to give them an heir. And if Kenny was tired of waiting after only a couple hours, I can only imagine how Abraham and Sarah must have felt after waiting 13 years. So they got tired of waiting for God to fulfill His promise, and they took matters into their own hands and ran out ahead of Him.

Sarah gave Abraham her servant Hagar as a concubine, knowing that if Hagar conceived a male child, the baby would legally belong to Sarah. And it must have seemed like a good idea to Abraham, because he did, in fact, conceive a male child with Hagar.

But look at all the problems that followed. The first was family discord. When Hagar found out she was pregnant, she began rubbing Sarah's nose in the fact. Sarah got so angry she mistreated Hagar severely, and Hagar ran away. She eventually returned, but the family problems weren't over. Eventually, when Sarah's child was born, Hagar's child tormented him. And how must Abraham have felt while all this was going on between his two wives and also between his two sons, both of whom he must have loved?

That's not all. The descendants of Ishmael (Abraham's son by Hagar) and Isaac (his son by Sarah) began to hate each other, and the enmity continues to this day—all because Abraham and Sarah ran out ahead of God.

You and I may not bring significant discord into our families or usher in generations of strife just because we run ahead of God (then again, we might!). But the point is, we'll bring some kind of consequences that God didn't intend, which we wouldn't have encountered if we'd just waited for Him. Put simply, you and I are not God, and we don't know everything He knows. We can't see the big picture like He can. Therefore, we are not the best judge of when the wait is over and it's time to move ahead.

I know it can be really hard to wait when it seems like there's no good reason not to go ahead. Believe me, I've been there, chomping at the bit. But I've learned through trial and error that when I rely on my own judgment, things don't turn out nearly as well as when I rely on God. So I've decided to wait on His timing, not only because He deserves my obedience, but also because I want the best for my life. And I'm sure you want the best for yours too.

The next time we are tempted to get going, but God hasn't yet said it's time, let's leave the front door closed. Let's wait until He's ready for us to move forward, and then let's go out onto the porch together.

Trust in the LORD with all thine heart; and lean not unto thine own understanding. In all thy ways acknowledge him, and he shall direct thy paths.
PROVERBS 3:5-6, *KJV*

REFLECTION QUESTIONS

1. Can you think of a time when you've run ahead of God? Were the results what you had hoped?

2. What steps can you take to make sure you don't run ahead of God next time you have to make a decision? Are you willing to take those steps?

19

Stop the Whining

In a totally unscientific poll I conducted among a completely non-random sampling of friends, I asked them to list the most annoying thing their kids do. I expected "whining" to top the list. I just knew it would beat out even things like kids' chewing with their mouth open and pulling the dog's tail, which you have to admit are pretty annoying (especially if you're the dog).

While the results of the survey were somewhat different from what I expected, they confirmed what I knew all along: Every parent has a pet peeve that really bugs the stuffing out of him or her. For some parents, it might be when their kids tattle. For others, it's when kids don't listen the first time they're told something (unless, of course, you're telling them you'll take them out for ice cream, in which case they can hear you merely *think* the words). For me, it's whining. I find that *really* annoying. Maddening, even. I would rather be stuck in a roomful of people scratching chalkboards with their fingernails than a minivan full of whining kids. There's just something about that *sound*.

I can think of two primary reasons why kids whine. The first reason is relatively innocent. Kids often whine because they're tired, hungry, sick or unhappy, and it's plain hard to be pleasant when you really don't feel like it. (Good thing we moms never have that problem, huh?)

The second reason is that kids think whining will get them something. Kids know that moms hate whining. They also know that it can be really tempting for a parent to do almost anything her kid wants rather than have to say for the thousandth time, "No! And stop whining!" (especially when standing in line at the grocery store). Buying your whiner a sports car (a real one, not a Hot Wheels), even though he is only five years old, could seem like a small price to pay for a little peace and quiet.

I've thought and thought about this pet peeve of mine, because there's got to be something more to it than just the sound. After all, we as moms endure thousands of unpleasant sounds every day just in the normal course of our duties. (I won't even go into those; it's annoying just to think about.) But none of them sets my teeth on edge quite like the sound of whining.

So if it's not the sound, what is it? Here's my conclusion: Whining represents a totally selfish attitude. Life is all about the whiner, all about someone making *her* happy and giving her what *she* wants. It's saying that if he's not happy, he doesn't care whether he takes others down with him. We spend our good moments trying to teach our kids a positive, others-focused attitude, so when they whine, it seems like we're back to square one. It's all about them again.

I guess that when it comes down to it, we can't be too hard on our children for whining, at least not without taking the plank out of our own eye first. That's because we as moms do the same thing. We make life all about us and our happiness.

We'll unleash our whining any time we're displeased, even when God's the one who's displeased us. If we're unhappy, we want the world to know about it, or at the very least, the offender. Granted, we usually choose more sophisticated ways of whining. We don't usually get the same tone in our voices as a kid does—though we certainly do that sometimes. Most of the time, we sulk, sigh disgustedly, or roll our eyes. Or we'll say nothing at all. Women are masters at producing silence or single words that can speak volumes. Oh, we may not express our displeasure in words, but we'll express it, all right.

I bet God feels the same way about our whining as we do about our kids'. I bet that if He were to use informal language, He might employ some of the very same lines we would say to our children: "What in the world are you whining about *again*?" or "Is that the kind of attitude I've taught you to have?" Or better yet, "My ears don't listen when you talk like that."

Life is not all about us, any more than it's all about our children. We would do well to remember that the next time we're tempted to whine. After all, what do we really have to complain about?

So a circumstance isn't to our liking . . . so what? Most of the time, we should probably just get over it. But if it's something more serious than that, praying about it would be far more effective than whining.

Maybe we're tired or not feeling well and having a hard time keeping a positive attitude. Complaining about it isn't going to make us feel any better, and it runs the risk of taking others down with us. We'd do better to pray or ask others to pray with us than spread the cloud of our negativity over others.

I know it's hard. It seems like we ought to be able to express ourselves when we're unhappy. And we can, as long as we do it in the right way. What's the right way? It could be a lot of things: prayer, talking with a friend, writing in a journal, going for a jog, or some other favorite stress reliever. But I guarantee the right way doesn't include whining.

So the next time we're tempted to whine, let's do what we ask our children to do. Let's find a positive, helpful way to express it, if it needs to be expressed. And if it doesn't, let's just let it go. I can't think of anything in this life where whining about it is better than doing something constructive. Can you?

Do everything without complaining or arguing.
PHILIPPIANS 2:14

REFLECTION QUESTIONS

1. Spend a day, or even an hour, keeping track of how many times you say something whiny or negative. Is it more or less often than you thought?

2. How might your personal and family life change if you were to spend more time speaking positive words, and less time speaking negative ones?

20

Shut the Door ... or Not

I am not a scientist, and I haven't done any formal research. But I firmly believe I have enough anecdotal evidence to propose a perfectly valid law of physics that no one else has ever proposed before (or at least, I haven't seen it in print). My law would read like this: *It is physically impossible for children who are playing outside to remember to close a door when they come inside.*

Actually, this problem applies to more than just our outside doors. Every door in the house is apparently constructed in such a way that a child is able to open it, but not close it. Especially the bathroom door. If I forget to lock it when I'm in there, I can be certain someone's going to come running in, ask for something or tattle on somebody, then run out, leaving the door wide open. After all, Mommy doesn't need privacy, right?

On the other hand, doors can be closed quite securely—and loudly—when someone gets sent to his or her room. Doors can also be closed to hide from Mommy's view what the kids are doing, such as smearing Desitin all over one's comforter and sheets. (Ask me how I know.)

Basically, the problem comes down to the fact that my kids leave doors open when they should be closed and closed when they should remain open.

Now, I understand that this issue is not a truly big deal in the grand scheme of things. I mean, so what if we donate a little extra air conditioning to the neighborhood? Why should Mommy care if she's trying to take a peaceful shower and four kids join her in the bathroom, all shouting at once? How much does it really matter if my kids don't know how to shut a door?

Probably not much when it comes to the kind of doors to which we're referring. Paying a few extra dollars on the electric bill is not a disaster. Getting Desitin smeared all over the linens makes barely a ripple in the stream of childhood. I can shrug and say it's not a big deal if my kids don't know how to open and shut doors properly, because eventually, they'll learn.

But there are other kinds of doors that it is vital that someone know how to open and close in the right way and at the right time. There are doors that stand open or closed between us and an infinite number of possibilities. If they're open or closed when they shouldn't be, they can lead us not to delight, but disaster.

I'm speaking, of course, of opportunities. Options. Possibilities.

You and I, in our limited wisdom, don't always know when facing a particular decision which door to choose. Both doors look the same. Behind one waits bliss. Behind the other waits destruction.

We need God to guide us in the paths in which we should go. He knows that two doors are never exactly equal, and He sees what lies behind each one. With His infinite strength, He can open or close any door He pleases.

What a blessing that He's willing to do this for us! If we walk up to a door and find it locked, we can recognize God's hand and gratefully walk through the other door. Or if we find the door open, we can rejoice in God's clear direction.

Sometimes, however, we deceive ourselves as to whether a door is open or closed. We approach it, turn the knob, and find that it opens easily. We exclaim, "Aha! An open door!" and run on through, despite the fact that the Bible tells us we should never have approached that door in the first place.

Or we tug on a doorknob, but the door won't budge. So we pull a little harder. Still nothing. We kick the door with no result. Next, we come at it with a hammer, and when that doesn't work, we use a battering ram. As soon as we breach the barrier, we say, "See? The door was open!"

Though we can't always trust our children to secure a door properly, we can always trust God. He will never leave a door to disaster wide open or fail to warn us not to walk through it. If we're seeking His wisdom, He's not going to decline to answer us, then stand by watching as we mess up our lives.

Likewise, He will not close a door that would lead to blessings for us. If God has closed the door, there's a reason. We shouldn't be like Jessica, my two-year-old, who, when she finds that Mommy has actually remembered to lock the bathroom door while taking a shower, beats on it and wails, "Let me in! Let me in!"

Even in our disappointment, we should be glad He's closed the door and protected us from whatever is on the other side, though we thought it was a good thing.

The next time we come to a door, let's ask God to make it obvious whether He's chosen to open or close it. Then let's either walk through it in joy or stay on this side of it in safety, and be thankful.

I will place on his shoulder the key to the house of David; what he opens no one can shut, and what he shuts no one can open.

ISAIAH 22:22

REFLECTION QUESTIONS

1. Do you usually seek indications as to whether God has closed or opened a particular door, or do you tend to step through whatever doorways look good to you?

2. Are you facing an important decision right now, and you need to know whether God has closed or opened a particular door? Have you been seeking Him consistently?

3. Has there ever been a time when God closed a door that you wished was open, but later you were glad He closed it?

21

The Money Tree

I have a money tree growing in my backyard. Fortunately, it's a perennial, so money blooms all year. Whenever I need more money than I have in the bank, I go out back, pull off a few dollars (or a *lot* of dollars), and go make my purchase or pay my bill. It's even better than an ATM, because there's no transaction fee, unless you count having to water it. I really think everyone should have one of these. In fact, if you contact me through my publisher, I'll be glad to send you a cutting so you can grow your own money tree.

Okay, not really. Please don't contact my publisher (at least, not for that reason). I can't send you a cutting because I don't have a money tree. But wouldn't it be nice if such a tree existed, and we all had one? Anything we needed, we could just go pick a few dollars, and it would all be taken care of.

My kids seem to think that's the way it works. I guess I can understand their perspective, since I usually use my debit card for purchases. All they see is my punching in numbers and getting to take bags of stuff home. Paying for things looks easy. Plus, as far as they know, I can always just drive up to an ATM and get more money if I want it.

Ellie actually suggested that one time. I had explained to her that the cost of a particular item was not in our budget. "Can't you just go to the ATM and get some more money?" she asked.

"Um, no," I said. "They take that money out of our bank account, and eventually, we'll run out, and the ATM won't give us anymore."

"Oh," she said.

Too bad it's not that easy to access unlimited cash. If it were, I'd have an ATM in my backyard. I'd plant it right next to the money tree.

I also remember a similar time when Ellie really wanted some toy we couldn't afford. "Can't you just make some money?" she pleaded.

"Well, Daddy goes to work to make money for us," I said.

"No, no, no," she said. Clearly, I wasn't getting the idea. "I mean, can't you just get a piece of paper and *make* some?"

"Actually, that's called counterfeiting, when you just print up some money in your basement. You can go to jail for a really long time for doing that," I said.

"We don't have a basement," she responded.

Obviously, something was missing in her understanding of exactly how one goes about getting money.

None of my kids has grasped the concept that our family doesn't have infinite resources, but I hope and pray they'll come to know the Someone who does. This Someone loves them even more than I do and always desires to use His resources for their benefit.

True, God will probably not plant a money tree in their backyard. My children will likely never be rich by this world's standards. Your children may not, either. But all of our children's *needs* will be supplied, and they'll be rich in the ways that really matter.

If we're Christians, you and I are already rich. Being able to connect with God directly and intimately through prayer is far better than having a money tree in the backyard. All a money tree gives you is dollars. Having a relationship with God Himself gives you . . . well, God Himself. We have a Father who perfectly cares for us, completely provides for us and comforts and supports us without ceasing. We have a Brother who died to make this relationship possible. We have a Spirit to teach us, guide us in the ways of truth, and instruct our hearts.

Not only that, but God has promised to meet all our needs. Not a few, not some, but *all*. And with His vast love, power and resources, He's capable of doing just that. Better yet, He invites us to come to Him boldly (imagine that—coming before Almighty God *boldly*!) to ask for what we need.

What an incredible privilege! We don't have to go to an ATM, which will eventually stop providing us with money, anyway. We can ask God to provide, and because He always keeps His promises, we can be confident that He will do what He's said He will do and supply our every need.

So the next time you need something, ask God to supply it. And then, instead of watching out the back window and waiting for the money tree to grow, rest in the knowledge of God's coming provision.

Considering how much He loves us and how many resources He has, why would we wish for a mere money tree?

And my God will meet all your needs according to his glorious
riches in Christ Jesus.
PHILIPPIANS 4:19

REFLECTION QUESTIONS

1. Do you tend to look to yourself (or your husband) to meet your needs, or do you look to God? Why or why not?

2. What can you plan to do first when your next need arises so that you look to God to meet your need?

22

Nice Earrings

I could see that Kenny was getting bored at the reception. Dressing up in Sunday clothes and standing around inside instead of getting to play outside was not easy for him as an active five-year-old boy. Nonetheless, his behavior was quite grown-up, and he looked handsome in dress clothes and a tie. I was impressed on both counts. But I thought he deserved a short break.

"Hey, Ken-n-n-y," I said, drawing out the syllables of his name. With a teasing look on my face, I beckoned him closer.

Kenny knew something was up. "What?" he asked suspiciously, standing right where he was, the corners of his mouth twitching upward into a grin.

"Come here," I repeated.

Wary but smiling, Kenny approached. When he got close enough, I reached out and grabbed him. He began to giggle, and I pulled him toward me and onto my lap. But I'd pulled him off balance, and in trying to keep from falling, he stepped on my foot. "Ow!" I said.

"I'm sorry, Mommy," Kenny said. "Will you forgive me?"

"Of course," I said.

"You have nice earrings," Kenny offered.

Kenny knew he'd hurt me, even though it was an accident. Because he felt bad about it, he tried one of the best ways he knew to make me feel better: saying something kind.

What a sweet, sweet boy. But even better . . . what a sweet, precious Father we have in God. Let me share with your heart, dear mom, what I mean by that.

The reason Kenny's comment touched me was not only because he was trying to be kind, but because inside me, like there is inside every woman, is a desire to know that someone thinks I'm beautiful. So when Kenny complimented my earrings, what I heard was,

"You're beautiful," and it met a need that's part of who I am.

I want to share something else with you, but before I do, I want you to know I'm not leading up to the same point people often make when introducing this topic. So please don't just turn the page and say, "I've heard all that before." Read on.

I know you've read or heard the Bible verse about how people look at one another's outward appearance, but the Lord looks at the heart. That's absolutely true, but it's usually used as a sort of consolation prize, to help us feel better about not being as attractive as we wish we were. *I'm glad God thinks I'm a great person*, we say to ourselves. *I just wish someone thought I was* physically *beautiful*. We gain some measure of comfort from the thought that even though our bodies can't be beautiful, at least we can be beautiful *somehow*.

But I want to suggest to you—and here's the part you may never have thought about before—Someone *does* think you're beautiful. Yes, you and me. And yes, *physically* beautiful.

We just mentioned a verse that talks about God looking at the heart rather than the outward appearance, but that refers to when He's determining a person's usefulness to Him. It doesn't mean He thinks we're beautiful inside and ugly outside. In fact, I think He sees us as stunningly beautiful outwardly.

That's absurd, you say. *He's God. He knows I'm not very attractive.*

But that's where you're wrong. And that's where I was wrong for so many years.

Yes, God is well aware that most of us aren't beauty queens by the world's standards. He knows what the world considers beautiful, and He knows that most of us don't measure up. Our noses are too big, our hair is too thin, our features are uneven, we're overweight, or whatever. People just don't think we're beautiful. But God does.

Here's why: His standards of beauty are completely different from the world's. He doesn't care whether our culture's standards say we should be tall or short, light-skinned or dark-skinned, skinny or rounded. It's irrelevant to Him whether curly hair or straight hair is "in," or whether we dress fashionably or plainly. What matters to Him is that He created each of us to be different, and we therefore each embody a unique facet of His creative artistry. To Him, that makes us beautiful and glorious.

In God's way of reckoning beauty, being gorgeous doesn't necessarily have anything to do with being 5' 10", blonde-haired, blue-eyed and a size 4 (unless that's the way He made you). As expressions of God's creative brilliance, we're beautiful even if we're confined to a wheelchair or bald from chemotherapy or we never had braces as a kid or our bone structure is too large or too plain. Our bodies are good and perfect gifts that come from above, because they are the ones He wanted us to have.

Granted, some of us don't take very good care of our bodies, and we should. After all, God only gives us one body, and we should care for it because it's His temple. But that doesn't necessarily mean we *won't* be plus-sized, or that we'll ever completely lose the baby "pouch." We're simply not all made to look the same. Our culture may try to convince us that there's only one way to look beautiful, but God says otherwise.

So the next time it's late at night, and you check on your sleeping son . . . and you stop and just watch him sleep for a while, thinking how beautiful he is . . . do something else too. Remember that God is looking down on you and thinking the very same thing. *You're beautiful, precious daughter. Yes, you. Both inside . . . and out.*

> *I praise you, for I am fearfully and wonderfully made.*
> *Wonderful are your works; my soul knows it very well.*
> PSALM 139:14, *ESV*

REFLECTION QUESTIONS

1. Do you struggle with feeling physically inadequate? Have you accepted others' assessment of you as not being beautiful?

2. Does it help heal your heart to know that you *are* beautiful physically? Are you ready to accept *God's* opinion of you as truth?

23

No More "Kay-ows"

Whenever we drive somewhere in the van, Jessica loves pointing out any and every animal she sees. "Duck!" she'll shout, when she sees a bird. Or, "Dat's a chicken!" (It was a rooster, but close enough.) Ever since she learned to talk, she's loved talking about animals. At almost two-and-a-half, some of her cute pronunciations are beginning to disappear, and I miss them. But I love the fact that she's still eager to spot and name all kinds of creatures.

Her love for animals also works as a great tool for distracting her from other pursuits. The other day, we were driving down a long country road in our minivan. Jessica was getting tired and cranky, and she began to fuss. Fortunately, at that moment, I looked out the window and saw some cows. "Look, Jessica! Cows!" I said in that overly enthusiastic voice we moms use when we're trying to make really, really sure our child gets interested in something.

Jessica followed the direction of my pointing finger and saw about 50 cows standing in groups or off by themselves contentedly munching the grass from their field. "Kay-ows!" she shouted.

Imagine the word "cows" pronounced with a really hick Texas accent (I can say "hick" because I'm from Texas), and you get the idea of how she sounded. It was really cute. But the cow distraction could only last so long.

Soon, Jessica began to fuss again. I didn't really blame her, because I know it's hard for a two-year-old to sit through an hours-long car ride. "See the cows, Jessica?" I asked brightly, hoping the bovine distraction would work again.

"No!" Jessica pouted. "I don't want to see kay-ows."

"Okay, then," I said, and shrugged. I turned back to the project I was working on, only to hear Jessica say, "I don't want to see kay-ows!"

"Okay!" I repeated. "You don't have to see the cows."

But Jessica wasn't finished. A few moments later, the topic mooed its way into our conversation again. "I don't want to see kay-ows!" Jessica sulked. "No more kay-ows!"

I turned to face her as best I could from my seat directly in front of her. "So . . . don't . . . look," I said slowly.

It didn't help. By this point, Jessica was offended that the cows were anywhere outside her window where she could see them. She wanted them *gone*. No more kay-ows, *period*.

As she kept fussing about those cows, I suggested several times that she simply not look at them. Finally, I gave up and let her fuss about those horrible beasts lurking *right there in the field* where she could *see* them. The *nerve* of those cows!

Never mind the fact that if Jessica had taken a simple action of which she was easily capable, the problem could have been resolved. She could have just stopped looking. But she didn't want to have to do anything. She wanted the offenders to be removed from her life without her having to act.

We adults often do the same thing, don't we? We complain about our circumstances, yet we refuse to take steps to resolve the situation ourselves. We act as if other people should have to resolve it for us—it's someone else's job to make us happy. At times, we refuse to do something as simple as overlooking an offense because we believe that the offender should have to be the one to fix the problem. But that attitude is as ridiculous as Jessica's complaining about the cows outside her window.

Yes, if someone sins against us, that person should ask our forgiveness. But realistically speaking, that doesn't always happen in life. It's far better to overlook the offense where possible than to keep staring at it, getting angrier and angrier, refusing to let it go because the offender hasn't apologized yet. Likewise, when we're confronted with unchangeable circumstances we don't like, it's far better to learn to accept them than to keep turning them over in our mind and railing against them.

True, there are times when it would be the wrong thing to do to simply ignore what's going on. But I'm talking about the times when we can, by our actions, make a difference in how the situation affects us. At those times, it's better that we act, rather than wait for someone else to take care of things for us.

It all comes down to this: we're here on this earth to serve, not to be served. Even Jesus, who of all people had the right to expect to be served, came *to serve*. It's not other people's purpose in life to make our lives easier. Yes, other people should serve us, just as we should serve them. But when it's within our power to change our circumstances, or at least our perspective on them, let's just do it, rather than hope someone else fixes the problem for us.

Let's stop looking at the cows, instead of expecting the farmer to come take them into the barn.

> *Then the LORD said to Moses, "Why are you crying out to me?*
> *Tell the Israelites to move on."*
> EXODUS 14:15

REFLECTION QUESTIONS

1. Do you do all you can to solve your problems, or do you wait for someone to rescue you? Why?

2. Does your usual response need to change?

24

The Strength I Need

Life got a little crazy when our third child, Lindsey, was born. At the time, Ellie was almost three, and Kenny was 18 months. So we had three under three. A few days later, Ellie turned three, but the craziness wasn't over. (It's still not over, in case you're wondering, though it's getting better.) One day shortly thereafter, my husband and I were sitting on the porch with our new baby, watching Ellie and Kenny play in the yard. It was a beautiful day, and we were enjoying the outdoors.

Before too long, a car turned into our driveway, carrying friends of ours from church who were scheduled to bring our evening meal that day. Three ladies got out bearing more food than we could eat in a week. (What a blessing!) My husband carried the food inside while my friends and I sat on the porch talking. Of course, they asked me how I was doing, and I admitted I was exhausted. I'd had a C-section, so that made things a little more difficult. I'd given birth less than two weeks before, and I wasn't getting any kind of decent, uninterrupted sleep at night. Plus, I had two young, active kids already. So putting all those factors together, I was pretty worn-out.

One of my friends, a tiny, petite woman with a smile like an angel, said comfortingly, "God will give you the strength you need. I know that sounds pat, but it's true."

I knew she was right, but I couldn't see how it was going to work out in my life. Was God going to allow me to get more sleep? Eventually, maybe. Was He going to make my two little ones start acting like big kids? Doubtful.

As time passed, I remembered my friend's words. And though I still didn't understand exactly how God was accomplishing what

He was doing, I realized that He was, indeed, providing me with the strength I needed. Somehow, I was able to take care of all three kids and get enough sleep, if not to feel rested, at least to function. Over time, life began to get easier.

But as I meditated upon my friend's wise counsel, I realized there *are* times when I don't have the strength I need to make things work out or accomplish a particular task. *Hmm.* If God really meant to give me the strength I needed, why did He only do it sometimes?

Of course, there's only one possible answer, and when I realized what it was, it made a huge difference in my life and even my day-by-day perspective.

God *does* give us all the strength we need. He's promised to do so, and we know He always keeps His promises. So, if God will give me all the strength I need, yet He hasn't given me strength to do a particular thing, the reason has to be that He never intended for me to do that thing in the first place.

Granted, there are times when the fact that we don't have strength is our own fault, because we fail to appropriate God's strength, which He makes readily available to us. If He doesn't make His strength available, it must be because our accomplishing that particular goal isn't in His design for us. Either God always keeps His promises or He doesn't. But we know that He does. So if that's true, He's hardly going to direct us to do something, then refuse to help us, is He?

Of course not. He's not going to command us to succeed, then refuse to help us, step back and watch us fail miserably. He's not like that. Yes, He may require that we struggle, but if His plan is for us to succeed, His strength will be there to help us make it happen.

The next time you feel like you don't have enough strength to get a particular job done or make it through a certain situation, instead of just trying harder, stop and consider something. Could it be that you're failing to appropriate God's strength? Could your struggles be the result of your failure to draw strength from the Vine? Or might you be trying to force an issue that God never intended you become involved in?

It turns out that God was ready to give me strength not only for three children, but for four. And He's helped me do everything I need to do for them. Oh, the house hasn't always been clean, and there have been times when I couldn't even find the kids' toothpaste, but I've been able to succeed in the way that really matters. I've done what God meant for me to do.

The LORD is my strength and my shield; in him my heart trusts,
and I am helped; my heart exults, and with my song I give thanks to him.
PSALM 28:7, *ESV*

REFLECTION QUESTIONS

1. Mothering can be draining. What do you do to make sure you have the strength you need to carry out your calling?

2. Most days, do you seek God, and His strength, or do you tend to rely on your own resources?

25

Uh-Oh!

When Ellie was two, her favorite toy was a Fisher-Price Little People Noah's ark set. She had the ark, complete with a flag, on top; Noah; Mrs. Noah; a box of tools, in case the ark broke down; a box of food, in case the animals needed to eat; and 10 pairs of animals. Ellie treated the animals like people. I wish I'd bought stock in Kleenex before Ellie received this gift, because I often found her tearing an entire box of tissues into tiny scraps to make pillows and blankets for her animals. Then she would lay them on their sides and put them to bed.

One day, Ellie was having trouble opening the ark. There was this little lever she had to depress, and then she had to open the ark while holding the lever down. At her age, Ellie found this difficult, so I did it for her. She took the ark from me and promptly (though accidentally) dropped it. The animals, which had been stored in the bottom of the ark, were scattered over the floor.

"Uh-oh," Ellie said, and froze, her blue eyes blinking up at me.

"Oops!" I said cheerfully, making a funny face, and Ellie smiled. We giggled together and knelt down to pick up the animals. Then, I'm sure, we probably made some Kleenex blankets for them.

Fortunately, the situation ended pleasantly, with our playing happily together. But it could have been much different. When Ellie dropped her toy and made a mess, she could have decided that the situation was awful and irredeemable and started crying right then and there. But instead, she did exactly what she should have done in her uncertainty. She looked to me. She knew that by my reaction, she could gauge how upset she should be about what had happened.

I wish I remembered more often to look to God for His perspective on a situation in order to determine how I should act. If I want my daughter to consult me, even with my limited perspective, how much more should I consult my heavenly Father, who knows everything? Too often, I respond to a situation without first checking in with Him and asking Him what His perspective is. And usually when I do that, I find that I've overreacted, or reacted badly. I've caused myself way too much needless worry, irritation or grief by forgetting to ask God how He sees a situation before I allow my emotions to rise.

Maybe you're like that too. Maybe you tend to react immediately instead of checking with God first. After all, we moms get used to reacting right away because of the very nature of our calling. We don't always have an hour to go meditate and pray about something before we decide what to do about it.

We desperately need to learn which situations we can handle on our own by using the wisdom God's already given us, and which situations are too big for us to manage without consulting Him right away.

At times, I've become upset and anxious about a situation I was facing only to discover later, when I remembered to talk to God about it, that God had it well under control and would have told me exactly what to do had I only asked. Maybe you've jumped into a situation with both feet and begun to make plans for damage control without first asking God to advise you on the true nature and extent of the damage.

Let's try something new together. The next time we feel our emotions escalating, whatever the situation is about, let's make it a point to *stop* before we do anything else. Let's check in with God and ask for His wisdom and perspective before we allow our feelings to cause us to do something we're going to regret later—whether that means damaging a relationship or simply robbing ourselves of peace.

Our understanding and perspective are incomplete. We are limited, finite human beings with the wisdom God has granted us, and no more. And He hasn't given any of us the complete knowledge and insight we would need in order to know exactly how to handle everything.

Only He possesses those qualities to perfection. And the only way we can be sure of knowing the right way to assess a situation is to ask Him.

To God belong wisdom and power; counsel and understanding are his.
JOB 12:13

REFLECTION QUESTIONS

1. Whenever something unexpected happens, do you tend to look first to God for His assessment of the situation, or do you form your fix-it plans without consulting Him?

2. Do you more often rely on your own assessment or on God's assessment of how to get through your day? (Think of the Word's instructions about fear, joy, loving others, and so on.)

26

Hug, Squeeze, Kiss!

What comes to your mind first when you think about the family traditions you enjoyed while growing up? Do you remember Christmas trees, special meals, or traveling to visit relatives?

One of my friends remembers hiking and fishing in the mountains. Another remembers vacations spent at the beach, with the smell of salt water in the air. My family's traditions were different from theirs, but they are nonetheless precious to me.

My favorite childhood Christmas ritual was getting to open one present on Christmas Eve. Our tree went up right after Thanksgiving, and the presents began appearing shortly thereafter. As each new gift appeared, I would check the nametag. If it was for me, I'd examine the present from every angle (but without touching it; Mom had a "hands off" rule), trying to figure out what the box contained. Finally, on Christmas Eve, when I almost couldn't stand the waiting any longer, I got to open one present. Oh, the delicious indecision! I would tear off the wrapping, find a wonderful gift, then spend the rest of the evening wondering what else might be in the other packages.

I work hard at trying to build traditions into our family life with our children. I hope the kids will remember some of these traditions fondly when they are older, and maybe even continue some of them in their own families. Already, some of our traditions have gone by the wayside, but there are some that look like they might be with us for a while.

One of their favorite long-standing traditions is called "hug-squeeze-kiss." It began as a simple, silly way to say good-bye, something I thought I would do just that one time. But somehow, that simple act gained a life of its own, and now, each time I say good-bye to the kids, they want a hug-squeeze-kiss. And apparently, it's become vitally important to my children's sense of security.

One day, I left with my oldest daughter to take her to a doctor's appointment. The other kids weren't around, so Ellie and I simply slipped out the door. My husband tells me that about 10 minutes later, Lindsey asked him, "Where's Mommy?"

"She took Ellie to the doctor," he said.

Lindsey fell to her knees, wracked with huge sobs. "Oh, nooooooo!" she wailed.

"What's the matter?" my husband asked.

Between huge gulps for air, Lindsey wept, "I didn't get to give Mommy a hug-squeeze-kiss!"

Lindsey had come to count on our simple routine to provide her with the reassurance that even while I was gone, we were still connected. When it didn't take place, she no longer felt secure.

Jesus knew His disciples would need to feel connected to Him in His absence. That's why He told them to wait in Jerusalem before going out to tell the world about Him. "I'm not going to leave you desolate," He said. "When I leave, My Father will send you the Comforter. He will always be with you, and He will guide you."

What a beautiful gift! Jesus promised His disciples God's constant presence with them. Even though He was about to die, the disciples would not have to be permanently separated from Him. They would receive His Spirit, who would be present with them for the rest of their lives, even though they couldn't physically see Jesus anymore.

Jesus' disciples were not the only ones who received that gift. Every Christian since has been blessed with the presence of the Holy Spirit. He reminds our hearts of the truth—that we are always connected to God, even when we can't see Him. We're intimately linked, whether we're in the midst of joy, tragedy, or simple busyness.

In fact, the Bible tells us that not even a sparrow falls to the ground apart from the Father's will. But God didn't die to redeem the sparrows. He didn't send the Holy Spirit to them. And if He is yet that closely connected with *birds*, how much more intimately involved is He with us, His dearly beloved children?

This certainty allows us to remain secure in the midst of anything. We know that our Lord's Spirit is with us, even when we don't see or feel Him. When the housework gets overwhelming, when our kids throw tantrums, when a friend betrays us or our husband forgets to notice us, we're still connected.

Being a mom can be lonely sometimes. Every mom I know—including me—has had times when she desperately longed for adult conversation and companionship. And it's true that sometimes we need a friend to give us a hug and tell us she's there, and everything's going to be okay. But though even the best human friend will be unavailable sometimes, or busy, or tired, God never will. He's always there for us—with us—*in* us.

And we know, as Lindsey knew, that one day, it won't be about trusting in an invisible connection until He returns. On that day, we won't have to imagine His arms around us, because we'll *feel* them.

One day our faith shall be sight.

But when he, the Spirit of truth, comes, he will guide you into all truth.

JOHN 16:13

Are not two sparrows sold for a penny? Yet not one of them will fall to the ground apart from the will of your Father. And even the very hairs of your head are all numbered. So don't be afraid; you are worth more than many sparrows.

MATTHEW 10:29-31

REFLECTION QUESTIONS

1. Have you entered into a relationship with God and received His gift of the Holy Spirit? If you're not sure, contact a pastor, friend or other trustworthy person who can show you what the Bible says about becoming a follower of Christ.

2. If you are a Christian, what does it mean to you to have God's Spirit present within you every moment of your life?

27

Seeing God

Back before I had children, when I was a part of the workforce and had a paying job, it was pretty easy for me to tell if what I was doing was effective. There were written procedures for me to follow, and there were clear, measurable ways of determining whether I was achieving the goals set for me. I naively assumed that parenting would be the same way.

Wrong! Or maybe a better way to put it would be, WRONG!!! With parenting, it's usually not easy to determine if what you're doing is having the proper effect. Sure, administering consequences might stop a particular behavior for the short term. But then our child does it again, and we wonder, *Does that mean I should be doing something else? Or will this eventually work?* Often it's only possible to answer that question in hindsight after enough time has passed, after we've done the best we could. Time will tell if we've reached our goal.

Knowing that we're doing the right thing matters enough when the goal involves some discipline issue. But it's *vitally* important when we're trying to make sure we're doing a good job of teaching our children about God.

We know we want them to grow up to know, love and serve God. But because our children are young and immature, we can't expect them to respond to our teachings in the way an adult would, so it's hard to tell if what we're trying to teach them is really sinking in. We're afraid that we'll get several years down the line and discover that we should have been doing something else, or doing the same things we're doing, but differently.

Fortunately, I've found that God graciously gives me an occasional glimpse of my children's spiritual progress to encourage me. The other day, the children and I were in our minivan driving home in the early evening. As we turned a corner near our home, we were afforded a spectacular view of the sunset. Honestly, I wasn't even thinking at the time about pointing out how God made the sunset. But Kenny was.

"Oh, look at the clouds!" he exclaimed. "God made the clouds!" And then, as if that weren't enough to show that his heart was spiritually minded, he continued, "I bet He *wanted* to make them. That way, He could surprise us." And then, with an incredible sweetness and gratitude in his voice, Kenny addressed his Father directly. "Thank You, God!"

"Yes, thank You, God," I echoed. *Not just for the clouds, but for the glimpse into Your work in my son's heart.*

There had been many times when the children and I had seen clouds, animals, bugs, grass, or a thousand other interesting creations. Often, I took the opportunity to point out how God made whatever we were looking at. I wanted my children to see not just a rainbow, but the work of God. I wanted them to admire not only a puppy, but God's handiwork. Whenever I asked, "Who made the tree?" they always answered rightly. "God made the tree!" So I knew they were receiving the information, but I didn't know whether it mattered to them.

On this day, I knew. Kenny had begun to internalize the fact that God is the Creator of all things. When he looked at those clouds, he didn't see merely a pretty display of nature. He saw *God.*

I realized something else too. I can do my best to feed my kids all the information about God that they need to know. I can remind them 20 times a day that God made this or that. But ultimately, for them to truly grasp that knowledge and move it from head to heart, God has to work. I can help my children put knowledge into their heads, but only God can put knowledge into their hearts.

I was humbled by the reminder that their spiritual development is not as much my responsibility as I sometimes think it is. Yes, I should take every opportunity God gives me to instill within my kids not only the factual truth found in the Bible, but also a love for the Author of Scripture. I must be a faithful example myself, so that my children will learn how to live for Him. But no matter how many things I do right—or wrong—only God can reach their hearts. Only He can cause them to desire a relationship with Him.

Only He can turn the sunset they see with their eyes into a glimpse of Him in their hearts.

Fix these words of mine in your hearts and minds; tie them as symbols on your hands and bind them on your foreheads. Teach them to your children, talking about them when you sit at home and when you walk along the road, when you lie down and when you get up.

DEUTERONOMY 11:18-19

So neither he who plants nor he who waters is anything, but only God, who makes things grow.

1 CORINTHIANS 3:7

REFLECTION QUESTIONS

1. Do you tend to see only the things God has made, or do you see God Himself?

2. Do you ever take personally the things God has done (as in, "that was for me")? How might your love for God be strengthened if you were to begin seeing His glorious works as intended not only for His glory but also for your enjoyment?

28

On My Terms

One of the best ideas I ever had was hiring my kids to do extra chores. I thought of this when I was in the latter stages of my pregnancy with Lindsey, my third child. I was tired from being so huge and from having two toddlers already (Ellie was approaching three; Kenny was almost 18 months). So I decided to see if Ellie would be willing to do extra cleaning in order to earn a prize. Fortunately, she was, and even at that age, she was a great little cleaner. So "Mommy's Prize Bag" was born.

I still have a prize bag today. Though the actual bag has changed many times, I still keep it on a high shelf in my closet where curious hands can't get to it. When one of the children wants a prize out of my bag, he or she has to do an extra cleaning chore that I assign. Sometimes, they request a prize; sometimes, I ask, "Who wants to earn a prize by helping Mommy right now?" Either way, it works.

I get to choose an area of the house that needs cleaning, and the child in question does it with a good attitude. He or she gets to choose and enjoy a new prize (all of which cost less than a dollar each), and I get a cleaner house. Everybody wins.

One day, when she was three, Lindsey came to me and asked if she could earn a prize.

"Sure. I have some cleaning that needs to be done," I said.

Lindsey began to cry and fuss. "I don't want to," she whined.

"You don't have to," I agreed easily.

"But I want to earn a pwize."

"Then you know what you have to do to get one," I said.

Lindsey moaned, her shoulders slumping. "But I weally want to earn it a diffwent way."

Hmm. Sounds like us and God, doesn't it? He tells us what we have to do to gain His blessing, but we try to find some other way to get it.

Even Moses, one of the greatest heroes of our faith, had a problem with this. God told Him to speak to a rock so that water would come gushing out. But Moses, having had it *up to here* with the children of Israel, struck the rock instead. Water came out, all right, but Moses earned the consequences of not being able to enter the Promised Land.

What's the big deal? we wonder. *Strike the rock, speak to it, whichever. What difference did it really make?*

The difference is that Moses decided to go after God's blessing his own way, and not in the way God had instructed. Moses failed to honor God's directions as to how to obtain it. God graciously granted the Israelites the blessing anyway, because they desperately needed it; but in His holiness, He also assessed Moses consequences for deciding to do things his own way rather than uphold God's honor before the people.

You and I are prone to do the same thing. We may not have any rocks to strike, but there are plenty of other things God has instructed us to do if we want to receive the spiritual blessings we claim we desire from Him.

Read your Bible, He tells us. *Spend time in My Word.* But instead, we read the latest parenting magazine, to the exclusion of having time to read Scripture.

You need to pray, He instructs us. *Spend time with Me.* Instead, we spend time with our favorite characters on television.

If we don't go after God's blessings in God's way, we're not going to have any greater chance at attaining them than Lindsey did at earning her prize without doing what I'd asked. In fact, we'll have less chance, because God doesn't bestow the infinitely valuable knowledge of Himself on people who aren't interested in taking the time to seek it.

If we really want the things we claim we want—a more intimate relationship with God, a better marriage, a peaceful home and well-behaved children—we have to go after them God's way. Doing things after our own fashion and expecting God to bless our efforts is completely unreasonable, especially when He's already spelled out for us a way that's guaranteed to get results.

So the next time we want something from God, let's stop and consider whether He might not have already determined a way for us to get it. If He has, let's follow it. If He hasn't, let's ask Him what His way is. To every blessing He promises to grant, He provides a pathway.

You want something but don't get it. You kill and covet,
but you cannot have what you want. You quarrel and fight.
You do not have, because you do not ask God.
JAMES 4:2

REFLECTION QUESTIONS

1. Do you want to gain God's benefits His way or your way?

2. Is there an area in your life right now where you're trying to earn God's prize your own way? If so, what do you need to change so that you begin doing things God's way?

29

A New View of Success

It just isn't fair. I'm talking about when you set out to clean your house—and I mean, do a really thorough job of cleaning and straightening—and it winds up looking a lot worse before it gets better. When I'm putting forth that much effort, I want to see steady, measurable results. I don't want to look up after two hours of hard work only to find that my house looks worse than when I started.

Such was the case several weeks ago, when I had determined that *this* time, I was really going to get things shipshape, and they were going to *stay* that way. (I know, I know, you would think that having been a mom for more than seven years, I would have given up on that idea long ago, but for some reason, I still have my moments of idealism.) Anyway, I had been working for hours when I stopped to take stock of my progress. And what I saw was not very encouraging.

There were piles of things everywhere that needed to be moved to other rooms or boxed up and put in the attic. In fact, there were more piles than when I started, and there wasn't much room left to walk on the floor in some parts of the house. Things looked worse. *Much* worse.

I found my husband standing in the kitchen. "I'm discouraged," I complained. "I mean, look at our house. There's no way I can get everything done in a *thousand* lifetimes."

"How can I help?" Phil asked.

"I don't even know what to ask for," I said. "It's like, I know I'm not going to be able to do it all, so why even try? I know I'm not going to be successful."

"You don't think you're going to have success?" he asked.

"No," I said, "because success is getting everything done."

But something—or better, Some*one*—in my spirit prompted me, *Is it really? Is that really what success is all about?*

As I continued to meditate on the Spirit's prompting, I realized that maybe success is different from what I always thought it was. Maybe it's not about checking off all the items on my mental to-do list in perfect fashion. Maybe it really *is* about giving my best effort and making my corner of the world a better place in which to live.

If I define success as "accomplishing everything I want to do," I'll fail a lot. But if I define it as "making things a little better," I can have success each time. That applies to cleaning. True, maybe the whole house isn't clean, but it's a little better than when I started.

I think that often I'm harder on myself than God is. Maybe you're the same way. I don't mean that our standards of holiness are stricter than God's; that's impossible. But I often expect myself to perform at a higher level than what I'm realistically capable of. God, on the other hand, knows I can't do every task perfectly, and He doesn't even expect me to. So why would I expect something of myself that's greater than what God expects of me? After all, He's my Creator, so He's intimately acquainted with my capabilities, because He put them within me. And if He knows there are some things I just can't do like I want to, and He isn't upset by that, why should I be?

Yes, it's frustrating not to be able to get everything done that I would like to get done. It's also frustrating that so many things won't *stay* done. So I have two choices: Either I can continue to strive for an unreachable goal, stressing out and stressing out my children in the process . . . or I can accept my best as "good enough," call it success, and move on. I could even use the extra time I formerly would have spent fretting about getting "behind" on things to develop my relationship with God, shower love on my children and help us make memories together.

You see, I've finally learned that success is not so much about reaching my own goals as it is attaining what God wants for me.

And what He wants may be far less as well as far more than what I intended for myself. Either way, it will certainly be far better.

> *For I know the plans I have for you, declares the LORD,*
> *plans for welfare and not for evil, to give you a future and a hope.*
> JEREMIAH 29:11, *ESV*

REFLECTION QUESTIONS

1. Does your list of what you "should" get done in a day ever differ from God's list?

2. Do you define "success" as getting everything done that God wanted you to get done, or checking off everything on your list? If you answered "checking off everything," what difference might it make in your life to define success as accomplishing God's list instead?

30

Why in the World . . . ?

Have you ever wondered why in the world you let your child do certain things? As in, *What could I have been thinking? How could that possibly have seemed like a good idea?*

For example, letting your child have a permanent marker when you're not going to be around to supervise what she marks. Or saying, "Sure, you can use the scissors." Only in retrospect, after we've seen the results, do we realize we should have done things differently. But by then, it's too late.

Take the time when I left a purple marker well within Jessica's reach. It lay on the coffee table, and I walked past it on my way to do something else. *I'll pick it up later*, I thought. Turns out Jessica picked it up first, sat down in our new leather recliner, and began to color. Fortunately, she only colored on herself instead of on the chair, but it took a week for the dark purple scribbles to fade.

Or take the time I was pretty sure Ellie was at least partially faking an upset tummy. The kids and I were having supper with my husband at his office, and we took our time getting ready to leave and loading up in the van. "My tummy hurts," Ellie repeated on the way home. "We're almost home," I said, more to pacify her than because I thought there was any real problem. But I was wrong, and I now know how much it costs to have the inside of our minivan deep cleaned.

All of us do things that, on later reflection, we can't see why we ever considered doing in the first place. Sometimes they're simply mistakes or innocent errors in judgment. Other times, they're sin.

The apostle Paul was well acquainted with this principle. He understood that even though we know better, even though at our deepest level we don't really want to sin, we do it anyway. The things we want to do, we fail to do. The things we don't want to do? Those are what we end up doing. Paul said he didn't understand why this kept happening to him, and we don't fully understand it either (see Rom. 7:15). *What in the world were we thinking?* we wonder. *Why did we do that?*

It's because we're still at war with sin. When Jesus came into our lives, we were completely forgiven of all our sins, past and present. Yet we still have to do battle with the habit of sinning. We have to put it to death, not just wound it a little. It's true that as Christians, we are new creatures in Christ. But that doesn't mean all of our habits automatically change.

We must be intentional about getting rid of our old ways, not just because we're commanded to do it and we owe the Lord obedience (though that should be reason enough), but because it will make a difference in the quality of our lives today and the way we live them. Jesus didn't make us new creatures so we could continue to live in the old way. He made us new so that we could walk in a new way. But we have to cooperate with Him in living as new creatures. He made us new; now we have to learn to act like it.

Most of us lock our doors when we leave home. We know we're not going to be home to protect our possessions, so we do the best we can in our absence. We don't want to take any chance that someone might enter our home while we're gone and steal our belongings. If we protect our material property to that extent, how much more should we guard our hearts and minds?

We should take every step possible to protect ourselves from sin's influence and from the influences of our old habits. If we think we can withstand temptation without doing anything to protect ourselves, we're sadly mistaken. Fortunately, the Bible tells us exactly how to do it. The first thing we need to do is to cry out to Jesus to save us from our sins. Then we should put on the armor He gives us—truth, righteousness, readiness, faith, God's Word and prayer. If we don't, we leave ourselves wide open to anything Satan tries to throw at us.

God makes each of us a new creation. He gives us a life where sin is no longer our master. "You don't have to serve sin anymore,"

He tells us. "Sin is out to destroy you, and I've saved you from all that. Here's what you need to do to protect yourself. If you do, you'll experience abundant life. If you don't, you'll be destroyed."

What in the world could we be thinking not to follow His instructions?

Put to death, therefore, whatever belongs to your earthly nature: sexual immorality, impurity, lust, evil desires and greed, which is idolatry.
COLOSSIANS 3:5

Above all else, guard your heart, for it is the wellspring of life.
PROVERBS 4:23

REFLECTION QUESTIONS

1. Is there anything belonging to your earthly nature that you need to put to death?

2. Are you diligent about guarding your heart and mind from sin's influence? If so, how? If not, what do you need to do differently?

31

Watching Privacy

I knew before my first child was born that things were going to change. We all know that, right? We know we'll get less sleep. We know we'll have to deal with all sorts of baby-related gear. We're well aware that the days of long, leisurely dinners with just our husband are over for a while. But we—or at least, I—didn't know some of the fine-print details about what was going to change.

For example, I didn't know I'd never get to use the bathroom by myself ever again. About the only way it happens now is if I sneak in there when nobody's looking and lock the door. Even then, sometimes they find me, and they stand outside calling, "Mommy! Mommy!" or wailing to be let in.

One day, when Ellie was about four, she saw me go into the bathroom. So she followed me. "Can I come in?" she asked, not waiting for an invitation.

"Actually, Mommy would like some privacy," I said.

Ellie gave me a quizzical look and responded, "But I want to *watch* your privacy."

For once, I was speechless. How does one respond to a statement like that?

See, that's the whole point of privacy—that nobody watches you. There are certain things and certain times we just don't want anyone else to observe. We want to choose what to reveal to others and what to keep to ourselves. If we're forced to let others see more of our actions or feelings than we want to, it's painful. We feel embarrassed. Vulnerable. Exposed.

We certainly wouldn't reveal our innermost selves to every single person in the world who wanted to know. No, *we* certainly wouldn't.

But fortunately, God *did*.

In Jesus' coming to earth as a human being, God laid Himself open and bare to our eyes. I'm not just talking about the fact that Jesus would have had His dirty diapers changed. I'm not even referring to the time when He hung on the cross, naked, for anybody who walked by to see. (He wouldn't have worn a loincloth on the cross as He wears in artistic depictions of Him.) I'm talking about how God laid His character and His heart bare in the person of Jesus.

True, God has always existed, since before time began, and certainly long before He created humanity. But until Jesus came to earth, we couldn't see God with our own eyes and live. We couldn't touch Him. We couldn't watch His emotions as He responded to the things going on around Him. We couldn't get so much as a glimpse of the members of the Trinity.

When Jesus came, He changed all that. He made God real and vivid to us. For the first time, we saw God. We heard His voice, we ate with Him, we rested with Him and we rejoiced and cried and worshiped with Him.

Yet the Bible tells us that we didn't realize who He was. We didn't get it that He was fully God and fully man until later, after He had risen from the dead. We didn't realize that God was *right here*, in our midst.

No, you and I weren't alive when Jesus walked the earth as the God-Man. But we can see Him even more vividly than His disciples did for the three years they followed Him.

Why? Because God still continues to lay Himself bare to us today through the person of the Holy Spirit. Though we can't see Him with our physical eyes anymore, He is even closer to us than He was to humanity then, because He now dwells within every Christian. We may not be able to see His earthly body, but we can still observe how He responds to things going on around Him. We can still learn from Him about each member of the Trinity.

Few of us take advantage of this incredible privilege the way we should. God has laid Himself out before us like an incredible spiritual buffet where we can taste His delights as He reveals each one to us, yet we settle for ordering a Happy Meal and ignore the lavish spread. God allows us to find Him if we only look, but we're not even looking. We think Happy Meals taste good enough, so we never stop to consider what might be on the buffet table. As C. S. Lewis said, "We are far too easily pleased."[1]

I want to see everything God has revealed of Himself. I want to learn all I can of Him on this earth, and then spend eternity learning more. I bet you do too. So let's go boldly into His presence as we're invited to do. Let's rejoice in the fact that He doesn't insist on privacy. Let's leave those Happy Meals behind and dive into the buffet. Will you join me?

> *We write to you about the Word of life, which has existed from the very beginning. We have heard it, and we have seen it with our eyes; yes, we have seen it, and our hands have touched it.*
>
> 1 JOHN 1:1, *GNT*

REFLECTION QUESTIONS

1. Have you ever thought of God as laying open His entire character to our eyes in the Person of Jesus?

2. When you look at Jesus, do you see God the Father? Try it. Look at Jesus and realize you're seeing the Father (read Heb. 1:1-4).

Note

1. C. S. Lewis, *The Weight of Glory* (San Francisco: HarperOne, 2001).

32

Heirloom

The loud crash and the sound of something breaking startled me because it happened right behind my chair. I whirled around to see Jessica sitting on the floor, wailing with fright in the midst of an overturned table, a heap of clothing that had been sitting on top of the table and a million shards of a broken ceramic bowl.

As I carefully picked her up out of the midst of the mess, it became clear just how many shards there were. I cuddled Jessica on my lap, stroking her hair to comfort her, knowing that my heirloom washbowl I'd gotten from a dear friend was beyond repair.

The bowl had been part of an antique washstand set. The bowl fit into the top of the stand, and a large pitcher sat beneath. It was the kind of set a person would have used long ago to wash up before there was such a thing as indoor plumbing. It was beautiful, and it had meant a lot to me.

I tried not to think about the loss as I checked Jessica over carefully and saw that she was fine. There wasn't a scratch on her. So I held her close until her sobs calmed down and then set about the task of cleaning up.

"Mommy, I'm sorry about your bowl," Lindsey said.

"Me too," Ellie said.

"Are you sad?" Kenny asked.

"Yes, I'm sad," I said.

With solemn looks on their faces, the three older kids tried to help me clean up the mess without my even asking. I knew they were trying to comfort me, and their efforts warmed my heart.

"Mommy, are you mad at Jessica?" they asked.

I stopped to consider my answer. No, Jessica shouldn't have been trying to climb the washstand. But she hadn't been disobedient.

She was just being a two-year-old. "No, I'm not mad at Jessica," I said. "She didn't mean to do it. Yes, I'm sad about my bowl, but I'm glad your sister wasn't hurt."

I turned to Jessica, who was sitting in the chair where I'd put her, watching me with a fretful look on her face. "Jessica," I said, "you broke Mommy's bowl, and I'm sad. But I want you to know that you are more important to me than anything in this house. You're far more important to me than that bowl. And Mommy loves you." I gave her a big hug. Soon after that, she felt reassured enough to get down and go play.

How different things would have been if, upon discovering my bowl broken, I had begun to scream at her. If I had gotten angry instead of sad, I would have crushed her little spirit. I also would have taught my three watching older children the lesson that when you do something wrong, you deserve to be yelled at and treated harshly.

But if I'd taught them that, I would have taught them the exact opposite of what our heavenly Father has taught us. Our offenses against God were far worse than Jessica's innocent mistake. God would have been completely just in letting us all go to hell as we deserved. But instead of screaming at us until we wailed in shame, He got down and cleaned up the mess Himself.

I mean that literally. He came all the way down to earth in the person of His Son, Jesus. Just as Jessica was incapable of cleaning up the mess she had made of things, so you and I were incapable of erasing the stain of sin from our lives. We'd taken the perfect life He gave us and shattered it into a million tiny, irreparable pieces. Then we sat wailing in the middle of our mess, completely unable to rescue ourselves. So God did it for us. He stooped down, lifted us out of the debris, and held us close. "You're important to me, because I love you," He said. And He swept up all the broken pieces we were responsible for.

But there's one important difference between what God did and what I was able to do. I wasn't able to repair the bowl. I had to gather up the broken pieces and throw them away. God didn't throw away anything. Instead, He took the broken pieces we had made and rebuilt a lovely washbowl. He took the mess and created something beautiful from it—something that's stunning, even though there are cracks, because those cracks illustrate where God's healing love mended us.

You and I aren't broken bowls anymore. We're whole. We might not look quite the same as we would if there was no sin in us or in the world. But instead of seeing our mended places as imperfections, let's look at them as glorious illustrations of God's incredible power to heal and restore.

You see, He's no longer angry at us. All of His wrath was satisfied when Jesus died on the cross for us. Instead of punishing us, He kneels before us and takes our hands in His. "You're far more important to Me than the mess you've made of things," He says. "And I love you."

When we were unable to help ourselves, at the moment of our need,
Christ died for us, although we were living against God.
ROMANS 5:6, NCV

REFLECTION QUESTIONS

1. Do you think of yourself as a broken bowl or one that's been made whole again?

2. Have you experienced healing from those things that caused cracks in your life? If so, do you regard the cracks as reminders of your sin or illustrations of God's healing?

33

Crumbs in the Icing

You'd think it would be easy to put smooth icing on a flat birth-day cake. Or maybe you wouldn't. Maybe you would realize that any birthday cake you attempt to make on the day of the party is doomed to some unforeseen disaster.

At least, that's how it seemed to go for several of my first few birthday cake attempts. Usually, I get them right now, and I can compensate for almost any cake-related difficulty. But early in my fledgling career as Birthday Cake Baker Extraordinaire, I made a lot of mistakes and spent a lot of time bewildered as to why my attempts hadn't worked.

The year Kenny turned two, he was in love with trains, so I knew trains would be the perfect theme for his birthday party. And a train cake ought to be easy to make.

I decided to make him a 3-D cake. It would actually look like an engine pulling a boxcar. Two parts to the train, two years old. It was the perfect idea. After all, how hard could making the cake be? It was mostly just rectangular pieces with a few square ones and some candy added for decoration.

But as with many of the good craft ideas I have had, this one turned out to be far more trouble than I expected. For one thing, the cake pieces didn't seem to bake evenly in the loaf pans. When they came out of the pans, they left a super-thin layer of cake along the sides of the pan. With the coating removed, I had to spread frosting over a crumbly cake. (This was before the days when I realized that freezing the cake before frosting it, or giving it a "crumb coating," would solve that problem.) So I got started. I mixed the right color of frosting, got out my knife (I didn't yet have an offset spatula) and tried to transform some lumps of cake into the train of my son's dreams.

After several minutes of trying my best, I was forced to admit there were going to be crumbs mixed in with the frosting, and they would clearly show through. There was no way around it. I sighed, sat back and looked at the pitiful cake. The engine was supposed to be blue, not blue with brownish-gray speckles. I needed some way to cover up my incompetence.

Then I spied the package of Oreos sitting nearby. I thought about eating the whole package to drown my sorrows, but I couldn't, because I needed some of the cookies to be the wheels on the train. *Hey, that's it!* I thought. *Maybe I can somehow use Oreos or other candy pieces to cover up the worst of the crumbs!*

It was a brilliant idea. Okay, maybe not brilliant, but at least better than telling everyone that Kenny's train had been out working hard, pulling its boxcar, and had gotten dirty. Somehow, I managed to glop on enough frosting and use the knife to nudge the crumbs into certain areas of the cake so that I covered most of the imperfections with the decorations.

Whew! It looked like a clean train after all.

With all the other preparations for the party that afternoon, I didn't think much further about the cake. But later that day, when I was thinking about what had gone wrong with it and how I could do a better job next time, I realized that what I was trying to do to that cake was a lot like what we Christians sometimes try to do to our lives.

We all make mistakes. Somehow, despite our best intentions (and especially when our intentions aren't good), we mess up. We wind up with sin showing through the righteous exterior we try to maintain. And we often compound our sin by trying to cover it up. We realize there's no way to make it right, so we come up with creative ways to hide it. We sweep it to one side. We cover it up beneath things that look a whole lot better. We try to make other parts of our lives so attractive that no one notices where the crumbs are showing through.

In fact, we may be so good at hiding our crumbs that all people see is a perfect cake. But we know the difference. And God *sure* knows the difference.

What we need is for our lives not only to *look* holy but also to *be* holy. Kenny's cake tasted as good with crumbs as it would have without crumbs. But it doesn't work that way when it's our lives that are filled with crumbs. They may look okay on the outside, but beneath the surface, behind the decorations, they're a mess. We need someone to give us a whole new cake and then frost it for us—someone whose abilities are far beyond our own.

In terms of our lives, that is exactly what Jesus did. Through our faith in Him, He made us new creatures. Our sins are gone—not just hidden, but also *gone*. Take just a moment to think about that. If you are a Christian, your sins are *gone*. Yes, other people might know some of the things you or I have done in the past. But when God looks at us in terms of our guilt, He doesn't see our crumbs. He sees only the perfection of His Son, Jesus.

What an incredible thought—that when God looks at my life, He sees me as perfectly righteous! He knows I've sinned in the past and probably will sin again in the future. But He no longer holds my sins against me. They are not only covered by Jesus' sacrifice on my behalf, but also they are *removed*.

This marvelous realization should move our hearts to profound gratitude. Our crumbs are gone! We're clean. In terms of righteousness, we look perfect.

And it turned out that Kenny's birthday cake didn't look all that bad either.

But you were washed, you were sanctified, you were
justified in the name of the Lord Jesus Christ and by the Spirit of our God.
1 CORINTHIANS 6:11, *ESV*

REFLECTION QUESTIONS

1. Are you still trying to cover up the crumbs in your life, or have you asked Jesus to cleanse you from them?

2. If you've never asked Him to cleanse you, why not do it right now?

34

Liberating Boundaries

When I was a girl, I was the proud owner of a bike with a yellow banana seat and those colored straw-shaped reflectors on the spokes. (Now you can guess how old I am.) I loved to ride my bike because I could go to the park, the community pool, or my best friend's house *all by myself*. The freedom was exhilarating.

My children love to ride their bikes too. Because we live on a quiet street where not many cars pass by, I often let the kids ride in the street while I sit in a lawn chair at the edge of our lawn and help them watch for oncoming traffic. I've trained them what to do if they see a car approaching or if I call out to them, and they're diligent about obeying.

I've also chosen a neighbor's driveway on either side of our house as boundaries beyond which the kids are not allowed to ride. I can see them easily if they remain within this area, and they are well within hearing range if I should call to them. Beyond those boundaries, I can't see them as well, and they may get too far away to hear my warnings. So I require them to stay within the area I know is safe—in other words, within the sphere of my protection.

God does the same thing for us. He encourages us to have fun in this life, but He also sets up boundaries beyond which we must not go. He chooses the limits of what will keep us well within the influence of what He knows is good for us. Beyond those borders lies danger, both physical and spiritual, from which He wants to protect us.

But let's be honest. Most of the time we see God's limits as confining, not liberating. We're sure that fun and freedom lie just on the other side of the fence, in the unexplored country.

We get it into our heads that freedom means not having any boundaries, and we start to resent God for imposing them on us. Then we either sulk while remaining within the appropriate borders, or we ignore them and ride right across, because the other side looks so fulfilling.

It's the same problem Adam and Eve had in the Garden of Eden. God laid out a very simple boundary. He said, "Eat anything you want except this one tree. Everything else I have made for you, but not this one" (see Gen. 2:15-16).

Adam and Eve obeyed for a while. But gradually they must have begun to wonder, *Why can't we eat* that *fruit? What's the big deal?* When Satan came along, they were ripe for temptation. It doesn't seem that Satan had to work very hard to convince them that eating the fruit was a good idea. I imagine they already thought so and only needed a little encouragement to do what they wanted to do anyway.

What they didn't realize is what we often don't realize—true freedom lies not in being allowed to do anything we want, but in knowing that if we just follow the rules, we *can* do anything we want without messing up our lives.

Isn't that an incredible thought? As long as we stay within the boundaries God has clearly laid out, we can do *anything we want*. Better yet, we can be assured that we won't mess up our lives or anybody else's.

If I allowed my children to ride beyond those driveways I've marked out, they would experience a certain kind of freedom they do not now have. Likewise, if we go beyond the limits God has prescribed for us, we'll experience a new freedom. But neither of these freedoms is the beneficial kind. Both come with danger and insecurity. Within the boundaries, we know we're completely safe. Outside of them, we can never be sure.

Which do you want? Do you want the kind of freedom that might be exciting for a little while but is certain to bring consequences crashing in upon you at some point? Or do you want the security of knowing that you can't mess up because you're within the sphere of God's blessing?

I know what I want for my children . . . and what you want for yours. We want our children to be safe. We want our kids to be able to explore to their hearts' content, but only if they can be protected while doing so. We're well aware that excitement is fleeting but safety lasts a long time.

God wants the same kind of freedom for His children—for you and for me. He *wants* to spread the joys of life before us and allow us to choose. That's why He's marked off the things that aren't to our benefit with yellow police tape. *Keep out!* it says. *You don't want to go here!*

Instead of resenting God for preventing us from doing what we want to do, let's praise Him for the glorious freedom He's given us. Let's thank Him for marking out exactly what's to our benefit and what isn't so that we can experience, freely and securely, the things that most interest us.

Let's stay in between the driveways. And let's be grateful we know exactly where they are.

The boundary lines have fallen for me in pleasant places;
surely I have a delightful inheritance.

PSALM 16:6

REFLECTION QUESTIONS

1. Do you think of the boundaries God has set for you as restrictive or liberating? Why?

2. Have you ever thanked God for showing you exactly where abundant life can be found?

35

Bananas and Motherhood

The thought occurred to me this morning that I have a lot in common with bananas. For example, bananas get eaten by monkeys; I get climbed on by four little monkeys. Bananas can be used to represent many different things (a telephone, a gun, a cheesy grin); I play many different roles (police officer, doctor, chaplain). Bananas are firm on the outside but squishy on the inside; I may look at times like a stern disciplinarian, but when my kids cuddle up to me, my insides turn to mush. You see? Bananas and I—in fact, bananas and all moms—have a lot in common.

Around our house, bananas don't usually last very long (that's where the analogy ends, I hope). My kids love fruit. Every week I buy a large bunch of bananas when I do the weekly grocery shopping. They're always gone within a day or two. Sometimes I buy a bunch that is slightly green so it'll last longer. But the minute the kids see those bananas show up on the counter, they start begging for some. The only problem is, green bananas don't taste very good.

On the other hand, overripe bananas don't taste good either (unless you make them into banana bread). As they start getting brown, their texture and taste change. None of my kids likes mushy bananas. The key is to eat them just after the green disappears, but before the brown begins to take over. You have to catch them when they're just right.

Actually, bananas are a lot like certain situations in life, too. Jump into them before you should, and they don't taste quite right. Wait too long to get involved, and they're rotten.

With a banana, it's pretty easy to tell if it's time to eat it. If you just look at the peel, you will rarely be surprised when you actually bite into the banana. But life can be a lot more complicated. We don't always know when it's too early to act and when it's too late.

Most of us tend to one extreme or the other. I tend to act too soon, because I'm an action-oriented person, and I hate to wait. I tend to get myself into things that I should have waited for, or never begun at all. Then I have to try to do damage control. One of my best friends tends to the other extreme. If she's not careful, she may wait too long to act and miss opportunities or have to make up for not having taken action sooner. Both of us love God and want to do what He wants us to do. But how do we—how does any of us—know when the time is right to act?

The answer's not easy, but it's simple. We ask God if it's time. We don't move before He says to; and once He does give the word, we don't wait.

Simple, right? So why do we get it wrong so often?

Maybe it's because we're not listening to God. We listen to our own desires and common sense instead of to what He might be telling us. We don't consult Him because the direction we should take seems obvious. But what looks obvious to us may have nothing to do with what God has in mind.

Then, too, sometimes we try to listen to God, but we can't tell what He's saying. So we get impatient and make our own decisions because we're eager or anxious to act. But when we act without His word, we run the risk of making a serious mistake. On the other hand, if we'd just waited a little longer, God usually would have made the answer clear.

Other times, we're afraid of what God has told us. Moses knew all about this. God told Moses He had chosen him to lead the children of Israel out of Egypt, and right away, Moses began making excuses and arguing: *Who, me? I don't speak well. Can't You just send someone else?* He was afraid.

Impatience . . . fear . . . rebellion. Is any one of these a good motivation for our actions? No. Yet we let them rule us far too often. Let's put all wrong motivations beneath our feet once and for all. Let's listen to God instead of to the directions of our own minds or hearts. After all, we're only the bananas. God is the one who made the bananas, and He knows exactly when their time is ripe.

There is a time for everything, and a season for every activity under heaven.
ECCLESIASTES 3:1

REFLECTION QUESTIONS

1. When you are trying to determine whether it's time to take action, do you listen more to God's leading or to your own desires?

2. Is there an area of your life in which you're afraid to step out and begin doing what God has called you to do? If so, what could you do to get free from this fear?

36

Keep Going

"What are you doing, Mommy?" Ellie asked.

I pushed back from the computer and sighed, stretching the kinks out of my neck. "Working on the book," I said. "What do you think I should write about?"

Ellie thought a minute. "I know," she said. "You could write about the time you put on the labels."

She was referring to the fact that a few weeks ago, I'd completely organized the children's rooms to the extent of making a place for everything and then posting paper labels (and pictures for the two who can't read) to show what goes where. That made it a lot easier for the kids to put things away properly when it was time to clean up. The system was working marvelously for us, and I was glad I'd done it. But it had been a huge job.

"What would the point be?" I asked, encouraging her to think.

"It could be about how, no matter what, you just have to keep on going," Ellie said. " 'Cause you just had to keep going and put on all those labels."

She was right. I'd had to stick with the job for hours until it was finished. It was a lot of work. But despite the fact that it took a long time to organize, putting on labels had been relatively easy to do. There are times in our lives as moms when we have to keep on going on tasks that seem overwhelming. Cleaning our kids' rooms, though somewhat daunting, is not that big a deal in the grand scheme of things. Other situations make it much harder to keep going.

One example is when we have a special-needs child. First, we deal with the grief of realizing that something isn't right about our child, and we receive a diagnosis (or have to pursue an accurate diagnosis from specialist after specialist). Then there are the medications, physical therapy or occupational therapy appointments, counseling (for the child and possibly for us and other members of the family), educating ourselves on our child's condition, educating others on the condition, enduring well-meant but ill-informed comments from people who are "only trying to help," watching our child struggle, and realizing that we will be doing these things for the rest of our lives. It's a huge task to come to terms with all that and keep going in the face of exhaustion, both physical and emotional.

Another time we desperately need endurance is when we're parenting our child through a difficult season in his or her life. We wonder if something's truly wrong or if it's just a phase. We struggle with consistency in dealing with the same behavior day after day after day when we don't see any progress. It's frustrating to be doing our best yet be unable to control our child's behavior on a consistent basis. We get "those" looks from other people, and we know they're thinking our parenting must be at fault. Yet we're doing everything we can.

Sometimes we need endurance not because anything's wrong but because we have many children, or we have them close together in age. When our third child, Lindsey, was born, our oldest, Ellie, was not quite three. Having three such little ones at the same time was difficult, especially since Kenny was beginning to struggle with some physical issues and was receiving multiple therapies. I was exhausted. I loved every one of my kids and I was glad we'd chosen to have them as close together as we did. But I was *worn out*. Then, just about the time that everything was under control, when Ellie was four, Kenny was two-and-a-half, and Lindsey was a year old, and I was back to my pre-pregnancy shape and jogging on a regular basis—in other words, feeling pretty good about life—I found out I was pregnant again. From the very first, I felt deeply blessed to be having a fourth child, as we had wanted a large family. But I was beyond tired.

Whatever the situation, it's easy to get discouraged when we've given all we can give yet we still have to keep going. When we're utterly exhausted, it's hard to keep ourselves on an even keel emotionally. During those times, it often looks to us like we might as well give up, because it's *just too much*. But, Mom, I want to offer the Lord's encouragement that you *can* keep going. I'm not going to tell you to just try harder, because sometimes, that's simply impossible. Instead, I want to offer you the words of the apostle Paul, who was writing to a group of discouraged Christians. He said, "Always give yourselves fully to the work of the Lord, because you know that your labor in the Lord is not in vain" (1 Cor. 15:58).

Most of us focus on the "give yourselves fully" part. *I'm doing that*, we sigh, *and I'm all given out*. But don't miss the second part of that phrase, for it's what gives us the encouragement to go on: "your labor in the Lord is not in vain." Wow. Did you catch that? Your work is achieving results. It *is*. It's *not* futile and pointless. It's not merely something that exhausts you and ultimately makes no difference anyway. Your work in the Lord is making a difference.

Paul doesn't promise we'll always see the difference. But he does say we'll always be making a difference, even if it's not visible to us. Even if everything we're doing looks like we're trying to hold back the incoming tide with our bare hands.

So when you're exhausted or at the end of your rope, and it doesn't seem like you're doing enough to make a significant difference, remind yourself of the truth that you *are*. It's Satan's lie that what you're doing doesn't matter, because God says otherwise. And He's the One who knows.

Always give yourselves fully to the work of the Lord,
because you know your labor in the Lord is not in vain.
1 CORINTHIANS 15:58

REFLECTION QUESTIONS

1. In what ways do you need endurance as a mom?

2. Did you realize that what you do as a mom matters immeasurably on every level?

3. Does it encourage you to know that what you do unto the Lord is *not* in vain?

37

If I Had a Dollar

If I had a dollar for every diaper I've changed . . . for every time I've said, "How do you ask nicely?" . . . for every time I've put a meal on the table in front of my children (which they liked yesterday, mind you) and heard at least two of them complain . . . I'd have $5,482,597,061. And I'd be writing this book from my own personal island in the Bahamas, where I live not only with my family but also with several maids, a cook, a hairstylist, and, oh yes, a whole team of people just to put those cute little umbrellas in my orange juice in the morning.

On the other hand, if I had a dollar for every time I've been critical over something that didn't really matter . . . or rushed my kids into the van when it would have been better to stop and look at that interesting rock . . . or said, "Mommy needs a rest right now" when they asked me to play with them . . . well, I don't want to think about how many islands I might be able to purchase with *that* money.

I usually award myself imaginary dollars representing times I've been annoyed or inconvenienced. But I might actually have *more* money if I collected bills for the times I've been annoy*ing*.

I'm sure glad God doesn't spend all His time remembering my offenses when He thinks about me. In fact, the Bible says that once we confess, He will never remember our sins against us (see Isa. 43:25; Heb. 8:12). Ever.

He's not up in heaven counting dollars and saying, "If I had a dollar for every time she (fill in the blank here) . . ." When He looks at us, He sees Christ's righteousness, purchased at a cost far higher than all the dollars in the world.

Most of us know this. We're taught from the beginning that when we're saved, our sins are for all intents and purposes gone.

That's what forgiveness means. But often we're not taught the other beautiful facet of this marvelous truth.

Not only does God grant us the marvelous mercy of removing our sins, but He also bestows upon us the incredible grace of remembering our sorrows.

I find the book of Psalms one of the most beautiful books in the Bible because in it, the psalmist holds nothing back. He pours out his heart to God, whether he's feeling joyful, angry or depressed. He lays all his emotions before the Lord and trusts in the Lord to receive those emotions and minister to his spirit.

In Psalm 58, David describes being pursued by his enemies. In fact, they had captured him. In a foreign country, in captivity and about to be put to death unless he could convince his captors that he was insane, he would have been suffering from far more stress than I usually endure.

David pours out his anguish and fear to God, asking Him to punish the nations standing against him. Then, he makes another request, this one is not angry but rather so poignant that I can almost hear him crying as I read the words.

Record my lament, he begs. *List my tears on your scroll.*

In Bible times, and still today, people record what's important to them. Just the recording of a matter grants it dignity and importance. Also, the act of making a record ensures that the person recording the information will remember.

This is important, God! David pleads. *Mark it down and never forget.*

And God does. For in the rest of that verse, we read David's rhetorical question: *Are [my tears] not in your record?* David knew he was asking God to do something God was already preparing to do—consider His child's suffering significant and record the details.

God does no less for us moms today. He sees our suffering. He counts it as significant. He records the details. But the amazing, absolutely incredible miracle of grace is that He is present with us in our distress.

Through His Holy Spirit, who indwells the heart of every Christian, God stands in the midst of our trials with us. Mom, that means He *cares* about what we go through. When we're so tired

from getting up five times in a single night with a cranky baby—
which we've also done for the last six nights straight—God is there.

When we're at the end of our rope in dealing with a difficult
person, God is there.

When our husband loses his job, when our child gets rejected
by a friend, or when a loved one dies, God is there. And He records
each sigh that escapes our exhausted lips. He marks down every
tear we cry.

So maybe, if I want to buy that island in the Bahamas, dreaming of dollars as payment for injustices I've suffered is not the way
to go. I bet I could buy far more if I had a dollar for every time God
has noticed my difficulties and cared.

> *Record my lament; list my tears on your scroll—*
> *are they not in your record?*
> PSALM 56:8

REFLECTION QUESTIONS

1. How does it make you feel to know that God not only
   sees your suffering but also is present with you in it?

2. Did you realize that God cares about your suffering
   enough to record each one of your tears?

38

"I Didn't Know That"

I love playing just about any kind of game you can think of. To me, a perfect adult evening would be spent playing softball, Monopoly, or anything else where someone keeps score. I even love playing Candy Land. Yes, still.

My children seem to have inherited my love for games. They enjoy all the traditional ones as well as some random ones I've made up in situations that begged desperately for something creative, like being stuck in a long line with cranky kids. One of our favorites is called "I'm Thinking Of . . ." I begin each statement with the phrase "I'm thinking of," and then I describe a person, toy, food or place with which my kids are very familiar. Their job is to figure out who or what I'm talking about.

One particular afternoon, Lindsey specifically asked for this game. "Wet's pway 'I'm Finking Of,'" she said. "Fink of somefing in . . . the baffwoom."

I was hurrying around that morning trying to get our day going, so it took me a few seconds to stop and change gears. "Hmm," I said. "Okay, I'm thinking of something that's large and brown and holds lots of things."

"Um . . . the light bulb?" Lindsey guessed.

"Nope, the light bulb's not brown," I said.

"The window!"

Obviously, something wasn't clicking. "No," I said. "The window's not brown."

"Give me a hint."

"It's *brown*," I repeated.

"The art box!" Lindsey shouted excitedly.

We've had the art box for years. It's a large plastic box containing the kids' art supplies—which, by the way, we don't keep in the bathroom. It's also very . . . red.

"Lindsey, the art box isn't brown," I said.

"Oh. I didn't know that," she said.

Actually, she did know it. Lindsey has known her colors for a long time now, and she uses this box several times a week, because she loves to make crafts. She regularly gets it down to spread its contents all over the floor as she prepares some craft, which is often a gift for me. She was well aware that it was red. *What in the world could she be thinking?* I wondered. Obviously, it wasn't that she didn't know the information. It had to have been that she simply forgot to take it into account.

I wish I could say I never forgot to take facts into account. But all too often, when I respond to a situation, I forget to consider the truth about that situation. Instead, I rely upon my feelings and desires to determine my response. Because feelings are always indicators of the truth, right?

Yikes. Of course not. And I know better than to act as if they are. But when I'm tired, angry or grieving, I don't think as clearly, and I'm not as likely to stop, think and then respond instead of react. Yet those are the times when I most need to take truth into account.

Let's say somebody irritates me. Immediately, emotions pop up that say I have a *right* to be treated better. I've been wronged, and I deserve to have the other person acknowledge it. If I act upon those feelings instead of considering the truth that it's to my glory to overlook an offense, I'm liable to make a mistake . . . sometimes a big one.

Or when I have to correct my children at least 5,000 times in the same day for the same offense, it's easy to get frustrated and disgusted with them. I wonder why in the world they didn't get it by number 4,999. It's not nearly as righteously satisfying to remember that God has had to confront me with certain sins in my life many times before I put them to death.

Truth is a lot more than just something that's nice to know. Truth *matters* in our daily lives. The application of truth can make a world of difference in our handling of a situation. If we learn to base our actions and reactions on truth instead of on wounded pride or a sense of what we're entitled to, we'll make far better choices in the way we deal with life. And even when truth doesn't change our actions, it may very well change our hearts.

Had Lindsey stopped to think about what she knew, she would have gotten the right answer in our little game. If I stop to think about what I know when I'm trying to figure out the right action, I'll get peace and joy. Best of all, I'll get God's approval. And the right answers in life are worth far more than the right answers to a game.

By the way—it was the linen cabinet.

Do you see a man who speaks in haste?
There is more hope for a fool than for him.
PROVERBS 29:20

Sanctify them by the truth; your word is truth.
JOHN 17:17

REFLECTION QUESTIONS

1. Do you tend to look for the truth in a situation, or do you allow your emotions to dictate how you respond?

2. How does this tendency affect your relationships with others? If it doesn't affect them positively, what do you need to do to change that?

39

Love Notes

Next to my desk hangs a red-crayon drawing in a simple wooden frame. It consists of leaf rubbings on a sheet of white printer paper. Around the edge, like a border, are several small rubbings. In the center is a larger one. "See? It's shaped like a heart," Ellie said when she presented it to me. "That's because I love you."

In a box in my closet is a packet of love notes from a not-so-secret admirer—my son, Kenny. One day several months ago, something inspired him to declare his love for me repeatedly, in writing. He delivered each note to me one at a time, folded up unevenly. "Open it and see what it says," he said each time. Each time, I unfolded the piece of paper to read, "I love you" or "Kenny loves Mommy" in his careful but irregular printing.

The same box that holds Kenny's love notes also holds innumerable crafts, cards and pictures that Lindsey has made for me. She often expresses her love by creating something unique and presenting it to me, along with a little piece of her heart. I have been the blessed recipient of many of her creations over the past couple of years.

You probably have treasured things that your children have given you. Maybe you have clay handprints from Mother's Day, carefully drawn stick figures of you and your child or a special treasure (like a rock or a pretty leaf) your child found and presented to you. Whatever the objects, I know you value them as expressions of your children's love, just as I cherish what my children have given me.

We receive other expressions of love on a daily basis. The only problem is, most of us haven't recognized them. Even if we did, we probably took no special notice of them. I'm talking about love "notes" from God.

Have you ever thought about how many times God expresses His love to you in a single day? He gives you the breath in your lungs, He puts food on your table, He gives you a place to live, He makes a beautiful sunset and spreads it out before you, He causes the flowers you planted to grow. Mom, these aren't just housekeeping chores He performs. He doesn't do all these things just because they are necessary in order to keep the world running. He does them as expressions of love for you. For me.

We all know that God made the flowers. But why did He make them so beautiful? Yes, He was expressing His creativity. But might He also have made them gorgeous and sweet-smelling because He knew we would enjoy them?

And yes, He has promised to meet all our needs. But the Bible says He *delights* in giving good gifts to His children. It doesn't say He does so as some sort of business transaction. He loves doing it.

I've tried to cultivate a grateful heart, and I think I usually am pretty thankful for what God has done. You probably are too. But let's take our gratitude a step further. When He does something for us, let's not simply thank Him as we would thank the cashier at the grocery store for ringing up our groceries. Let's stop and realize that His giving is an expression of His love, and let's thank Him for *that* too.

How beloved would we feel if we began to notice the myriad expressions of love God shows us every day? I bet we wouldn't even be able to count them all. The comfortable pillow you laid your head on to sleep last night? Yep. He loves you. The delicious bowl of oatmeal I ate this morning? Yep. He loves me.

We're not going to feel all that loved if we don't recognize it when God shows His love for us. We know that He loves us in a general kind of way, and we're grateful for that. But He loves us very specifically too. And He shows it every day.

I'm going to keep that crayon drawing and those love letters and those crafts my whole life. But I'm going to keep God's love for eternity. And I'm ready to start enjoying it now. Aren't you?

*What is man that you are mindful of him, and the son of man that you care
for him? Yet you have made him a little lower than the heavenly beings and
crowned him with glory and honor. You have given him dominion over
the works of your hands; you have put all things under his feet.*

PSALM 8:4-6, *ESV*

REFLECTION QUESTIONS

1. Do you tend to think of God's love in a general sense,
   or do you see it in the details of your life?

2. How many different, specific ways can you think of
   that God has shown His love to you today?

40

It's the Journey

The other day I was actually out running errands (are you ready for this?) *by myself.* My husband was at home with the kids, so I took the chance to get several things done. That's what my "alone time" usually consists of now—trips to do errands. But I don't mind. I like getting to go spend money.

So I went to five different places to buy or return things. I wasn't hurrying, just moving efficiently, and it felt like I was getting a lot done. But until I looked at my watch and saw that only an hour had passed, I had no idea just how efficient I was.

Granted, I used to be able to run errands quickly and efficiently, so this wasn't a new skill. But it has been so long since I was able to do it on a regular basis that when it happens, it always surprises me.

I looked at my watch again. It showed the same time as it had a second ago. I calculated when I had arrived at the first store and subtracted. One hour, indeed.

There's a parallel for this in the world of exercise and sports. You know how athletes sometimes train with weights strapped to their bodies while they're running or doing aerobics or whatever? The idea is that if they can train their bodies to excel *with* the weights, then once they take the weights off, they'll be even faster and have more endurance. My day of running errands was kind of like that. I felt like I was no longer slogging through quicksand but running like the wind. And it was a really nice feeling.

I must admit that I began to feel vaguely guilty for being so glad the kids weren't with me. Often, I enjoy having them along; that particular time, I didn't want them there. I wanted to be free to get things done at my own pace without being slowed down.

I didn't want the weights on my ankles (sometimes literally). I wanted to feel lighter and faster than I would have felt if the children were with me.

But then, pulling into the parking lot at Target, a question flashed into my mind. *When I have the kids along, what am I really trying to accomplish, anyway? Am I trying to pick up groceries from Target, or am I trying to teach them about life?*

Most of the time, it's the "groceries from Target" option. I don't always think about teaching my children when we're out and about unless they do something wrong or I need to give them instructions. But whether I do it purposefully or not, I am teaching them constantly. When they see my attitude as I go about my work, or they hear me speak nicely to the cashier, or they see me react when the store is out of something I wanted to buy, they are learning. And if all I'm trying to accomplish is filling the cart with groceries, I'm missing opportunities that are far more valuable than stocking the pantry.

I can either teach the kids how not to annoy me when I'm trying to hurry through a shopping trip, or I can teach them that they are valuable and precious members of our family, and that I love being with them.

I can act as if the ultimate goal of our being together is getting something done, or I can show them that just being together is good, even if we don't accomplish much.

Sure, sometimes I'd love to be able to simply do errands without trying to teach life lessons. But that's not the way it works. I'm teaching, whether I like it or not. So I might as well accept that fact and think about what lessons I consider the most important to teach.

I want my kids to learn that when you open your door in the parking lot and the wind blows it out of your hand, and it significantly dents the vehicle next to you, you leave a note with your name and phone number under the windshield wiper, promising that if the owner calls you, you will make everything right. (Don't ask me how I know this one. But at least my oldest daughter still remembers that I acted with integrity at the time.)

I want them to learn that we notice service people such as the cashier. We don't treat them like they're invisible. We call them by name or start a friendly conversation with them, recognizing that they're people who are just as important as we are.

There are many other potential learning opportunities, and it seems like new ones arise every day. But ultimately, what I want the kids to remember most about running errands together is that it was fun to be with Mommy and each other. I want them to remember us enjoying each other wherever we were—not constantly getting hustled in and out of stores because they were slowing me down.

You see, I've realized that it's not about the destination. In the long run, it won't matter if my kids and I get everything on the list done or not. It's about the journey. And it *will* matter what I taught them along the way.

These words that I command you today shall be on your heart.
You shall teach them diligently to your children, and shall talk
of them when you sit in your house, and when you walk by the way,
and when you lie down, and when you rise.
DEUTERONOMY 6:6-7, *ESV*

REFLECTION QUESTIONS

1. Are you diligently teaching your children about God? If not, what are some ways you might do this?

2. How could you turn your next shopping trip into an opportunity to teach your children more than just how to run errands?

41

"Yes!"

I love it when I get brownie points with the kids for surprising them. So a couple months ago, I decided to build up a little suspense before taking them to an activity I knew they would enjoy.

All four kids were in the playroom. "Hey, kids! I have an idea," I said excitedly. "Oh, but wait a minute." I really had their attention now. "You look like you're having fun playing. You might not want to do it," I said.

"What's your idea?" Kenny asked.

"Well, you're having fun playing. You might not want to—"

"Yes!" Kenny said. "I do!"

"Wait till I tell you what it is," I said. "We can either stay here and play—"

"No!" Kenny interrupted.

"Or . . ." and I explained to them about the fun activity.

"Yea!" they shouted. "Let's go!" They ran past me and out of the room to get their shoes on and go potty—all the things they do as part of their "going somewhere" routine.

I knew they would like my plan, so their reaction wasn't too surprising. What was most notable to me was Kenny's eagerness to agree to my plan before he knew what it was.

We as moms should do the same thing when it comes to God's plans: we should agree with them even before we know what they are. True, Kenny is not enthusiastic about some of my plans, and we probably won't like some of God's, either. But we shouldn't base our willingness to follow on whether or not they sound like fun.

The biblical patriarch Abraham knows just what I'm talking about. When he got his instructions from God, all God said was, "Leave here and go somewhere else. I'll tell you later where it is that you're going."

Abraham could have argued with God. "I can't do that without knowing some details. How many supplies should I take with me? What if they run out before we get there? How will I take care of my family along the way? What if we try to stop somewhere and the hotel doesn't allow camels?"

Those sound like reasonable questions to a human way of thinking. But God doesn't have a human way of thinking, and He wants us to trust His thinking and not our own.

We're not likely to have to travel to a foreign country without knowing where we're going or the route we'll take to get there. That would probably be impossible these days, anyway. But God does sometimes ask us to do things that are equally huge.

Maybe He gives us the assignment of parenting a special-needs child. *God, I don't know anything about this kind of parenting. This wasn't what I wanted for my son's life. What am I going to do?*

Or maybe He asks us to remain in a marriage that isn't all we hoped it would be. *God, how am I supposed to stay? All he does is sit in front of the television. He never talks to me.*

From an earthly perspective, it would be completely understandable and even reasonable for us to respond, *No way, God. I'm not doing this.* But from God's heavenly perspective, He's leading us to a better country.

Can it really be better to do something painful that God asks of us than to relieve our pain by making our own plans? Yes. And I guarantee that if God is asking us to do something, it is *definitely* better to obey than to go our own way. Too often, we define "better" as "the absence of pain." But we're not always right. Sometimes there has to be pain before we can get to the good on the other side. If we get out of the situation now, we might avoid some of the pain. But we'll never reach the better country we would have dwelt in had we traveled God's way.

I know it's hard to say yes in advance. We fear that by saying yes, we'll be letting ourselves in for some pain we could avoid by saying no. But *not* going along with God's plan is ultimately what is most painful.

Let's not let our fear of what's ahead cause us to say no to participating in God's plan. When He lets us know He has a plan in a certain area for us, may we be willing to say "Yes!" as Kenny did—immediately and without hesitation. It may not always be fun, but it will always be the best choice.

The LORD *had said to Abram, "Leave your country, your people and your father's household and go to the land I will show you."*
GENESIS 12:1

REFLECTION QUESTIONS

1. Do you prefer to have all the details before you strike out in a new direction? Why or why not?

2. Is there a new direction God's asking you to go? Are you willing to go without knowing all the details? If not, why not?

42

Where We Don't Belong

I knew it couldn't possibly bode any good when Ellie went into the bathroom to use the potty, lifted the lid and stood there staring. "Hey, Mommy! Come see this!" she called. "You're going to think this is really funny."

Yikes. *Funny* wasn't a word I'd ever thought would be mentioned in the same breath as our toilet. Cringing, I slowly pushed back from the desk, stood up, and walked into the bathroom.

Ellie pointed into the toilet bowl. There was Jessica's small stuffed duck perched on top of a piece of cardboard that was obviously the back of a package of something. The package was wedged into the potty in such a way that the little duck smiled up at us from her comfortable perch just above the water line.

Shaking my head and grinning—I couldn't help it—I gingerly lifted the duck off the cardboard. Nope, she wasn't wet. I set her on the vanity and reached for the cardboard. Well, nuts. Now that the duck was out of the potty, I could see that the cardboard-backed package contained an eraser and some dry-erase markers I'd intended to return to the store. I reached in and picked up the package by its one dry corner. Water poured from it. Nope, there would be no returning it now.

"Isn't that funny, Mommy?" Ellie asked.

"Yes, it's pretty funny, sweetheart," I said, allowing myself to chuckle at the absurdity of it.

Right about then, Jessica walked in.

"Jessica, did you put your duck and this package in the potty?" I asked.

"Yes," she said proudly, grinning one of her toothy grins.

The three of us had a good laugh together, and the story remains one of my favorites to this day. I just love the unexpectedness of finding a duck, some markers and an eraser in the potty. It's funny, it's sweet, and (hopefully) it's a one-time event.

But it's not always funny when things are out of place. Sometimes it's annoying, disturbing, or even tragic. At the very least, it's a disruption of God's plan for the way things were supposed to be.

When we insist on trying to pursue our own desires even when they run contrary to God's desires, we put ourselves in a place where we don't belong. Maybe we've pursued a career that's wrong for us, knowing that God doesn't intend for us to be in that particular marketplace. But because we wanted to be there, we've forced our way in, despite the fact we belong there about as much as a stuffed duck belongs in a toilet. Or perhaps we've always longed for whatever we count as success in a particular arena, so we've devoted ourselves to pursuing it, only to find that we belong there as much as dry-erase markers belong in a potty.

Why is it that we try so hard to belong in places we were never meant to be? Usually, it's because we want so badly to be there. But what we've all failed to realize at one time or another is that it's not being where *we* want that brings the fulfillment and satisfaction we seek; it's being where *God* wants us to be.

You see, God has designed and equipped us to fulfill a particular role in this world. If we spend all our time trying to be somewhere else or do some*thing* else, not only will we probably experience dissatisfaction in the place we weren't meant to be, but we'll also miss out on the rich blessings God had planned to give us in the *place* He planned for us to be.

Oh, sure, the other side of the fence might look greener, but it's an optical illusion. It's not really a field full of green grass; it's a field planted with grass that Satan has painted to look green so he can deceive us into moving to his side of the fence. And when we get there, we'll find that in pursuing what we thought was the best, we've cheated ourselves out of what the best really was.

I don't know how you feel about yourself, but I'm certain that the best I can think of for myself pales in comparison to the best

God has in mind for me. I'd rather trust His judgment on which grass is greener. After all, if He says that His side of the fence is greener than the other side, I'd rather believe Him than trust my own eyes. Wouldn't you?

As the heavens are higher than the earth, so are my ways higher than your ways and my thoughts than your thoughts.
ISAIAH 55:9, *ESV*

REFLECTION QUESTIONS

1. Are you filling the role God intends for you to fill? If not, what do you need to do to begin walking in obedience?

2. If you're not sure what role you're supposed to be filling, how might you go about finding out?

43

All Planned

Okay, I'll confess: I absolutely love grocery shopping. Most moms I know could take it or leave it—preferably leave it—but for me, grocery shopping is one of the highlights of my week. Basically, it comes down to the fact that I get to go buy a ton of stuff and spend money without feeling guilty about it. It also doesn't hurt that my husband stays home with the kids while I get some time to myself.

One particular week, I did the shopping late on a Sunday evening. By the time I got home and pulled into the driveway, it had been dark for a while. As I put the car into park, the front door opened, and light came spilling out, along with two of my daughters. Ellie and Lindsey greeted me on the front porch in their jammies. "Mommy! You're home! We'll help you bring the groceries in."

"Stay up there," I said, as they started to head down the steps in their bare feet. "I'll bring the bags onto the porch, and you can carry them into the house."

"We'll come get the bags," Ellie said, continuing toward me, not daunted in the slightest.

"The rocks might hurt your feet," I explained. (We have a gravel driveway.)

But Ellie bounded down off the porch and began picking her way across the stepping-stones to the driveway. She loves to help, and she's a great helper. "Don't worry," she said. "We've got it all planned."

I sighed. I appreciated their helpful spirits, but at that point, what I wanted more than help with the groceries was their obedience—their willingness to do things my way.

I bet God feels the same way in dealing with us sometimes. I can just imagine the look on His face when *we* not only tell *Him* the areas where we're going to serve Him, but then take it a step further and tell Him how we're going to do it.

What God wants is not for us to strike out on our own, jumping feet first into whichever opportunities we think He would most appreciate. He wants us to offer ourselves for His service and ask *Him* what He wants us to do. We often act as if any opportunity that presents itself must be what God wants; so we sign up for it and then wonder why it turns out to be such a burden. Could it be because that was never what He had in mind for us?

Or worse yet, we jump into a particular opportunity because *we* want to, without any regard for what God might want. At least when we think God wants something, we're trying to obey Him. But when we operate as if what we want is the primary motivating factor in choosing our areas of service, we do Him a grave disrespect.

True, God often calls us to areas in which we have an interest. In fact, He put those interests within us to help us succeed at what He's planning on calling us to do. But we act like our interests are an end in themselves instead of a means to an end.

Sometimes we take it a step further. We not only tell Him where we're going to serve, we tell Him *how* we're going to do it. And when He tries to correct us, we ignore Him. We pay lip service to respect for His desires, but our actions show contempt. Most of us would never say that God's desires don't matter to us. But when we go off on our own, doing our own thing without bothering to consult Him, and without listening to Him when He does speak, we're showing disrespect by our actions.

How frustrated He must get when He tells us to do things a particular way and we insist that our own way is better! The Bible is full of commandments that we don't obey because we don't want to or we think we have a better way. Maybe you've been guilty of some of these things, as I have.

For example, God commands us, "Speak the truth in love," and we transform that into, "I'll speak, all right." Or He says,

"Learn to die to yourself," and we think, "That doesn't work in to-day's world. I'll get walked on."

If only we would believe that God really does know best, and determine to seek His will and then obey it.

He may not want us to carry in the groceries at all, and if we insist on doing it, we'll miss the greater blessing He had planned. Or He may allow us to carry them in, but if we insist on doing it our way, the task will be more difficult than if we had done it His way.

In either case, it should be up to Him whether we carry the bags, and if so, how. Let's wait on the porch, ask Him if He wants our help, and then—if He does—do the job His way.

Does the LORD delight in burnt offerings and sacrifices as much as
in obeying the voice of the LORD? To obey is better than sacrifice,
and to heed is better than the fat of rams.

1 SAMUEL 15:22

REFLECTION QUESTIONS

1. When you feel a desire to serve, do you check with God to see if He wants you to act upon it, or do you tend to jump right into service?

2. Is there an area in which you currently serve where you need to ask God if you are serving in the way He wants you to?

3. Is there a particular area where you're not currently serving, but you would like to serve? Why not ask God if He'll make a way for you to serve there?

44

Hampers

It's not every day you see a clothes hamper grow legs and chase after you. Or maybe it is. I guess it all depends on what goes on at your house. But in our house, this only happens occasionally.

The other day, I was sitting at the computer, working on this manuscript, when I heard footsteps, then a thump. I looked, and there, behind me, was an upside-down clothes hamper that hadn't been there a moment ago. "Mommy, find me," the hamper said.

"Oh, Lindseyyyy! Where are youuuuu?" I sang out cheerfully. I pretended to look everywhere for her, finally finding her in—you guessed it—the hamper. She giggled and wanted to play it again.

At about that moment, another hamper entered the room. It plunked down on the floor beside the first one. "Find *me*," it said. So I looked everywhere for Kenny, and would you believe I found him inside the second hamper?

Eventually, Jessica got in on the game. (Fortunately, we have plenty of hampers.) For a while, we played find-the-kid-in-the-hamper. Then the game morphed into something different. I had gotten up to go get a snack when I noticed something. One of the hampers had grown legs, and it was following me! Pretty soon, the other two grew legs as well, and all three hampers were bumping into each other and wobbling as they pursued me into the kitchen.

"Aaaahhh!" I pretended to scream. "Daddy, I have three hampers chasing me!"

Fortunately, the giggling hampers had holes in them, so the kids were able to see reasonably well as they chased me through the kitchen and into the living room.

But even after the game was over, the kids still continued to play with the hampers. In fact, we have a picture of two hampers

with legs that look suspiciously like Kenny's and Lindsey's, standing at the front door watching for the ice cream truck to come by.
It turns out those hampers are almost as good as cardboard boxes
for generating fun.

It was a crazy, fun day of playing in a way I'd never thought
of before.

Actually, we have lots of moments like that, and I'm glad.
The details differ from time to time, but we have lots of instances
of good, quirky fun. And those are the things that make good
memories.

When my kids are grown up, I want them to remember that we
had fun together. I want them to think about the times they played
dress-up, or we all ate outside in their little playhouse, or spent a
week playing games made up with hula hoops. Who knows?
Maybe one day, Kenny will even say, "Hey, Lindsey, remember that
day we put the hampers on our heads and chased Mom around
the house?"

Or maybe he'll forget the hamper incident but remember
something else equally crazy and fun. Either way, I'm fine with
that. I just want them all to remember fun as being a part of our
family's structure, an integral part of who we are.

I want them to know something else too. "Hey, do you know
who invented fun?" I asked once, after our laughter over some zany
incident had subsided enough for me to catch my breath.

"Who?" they asked.

"God did."

I want them to know that fun was not something human beings thought up. It was invented by the Author of fun; He gave it
to us as a gift to make our lives more enjoyable. And because God
is infinitely creative, fun can crop up at any time and in unexpected ways. I want my kids to be ready for that. And when they
have fun, I want them to realize who provided it for them, and acknowledge it as one of His greatest gifts.

Actually, I want one more fun-related thing for them. I want
them to keep having fun their whole lives, and not stop just because they think they get too old for it. God didn't plan for us to

have fun as children, and then grow up to have boring adult lives. I believe He intended for us to have lifelong fun. Sure, some of the ways we have fun may change. I don't get nearly as much enjoyment out of throwing my food on the floor as I surely did when I was a toddler. But instead of giving up fun, we should find new, creative ways to have it.

So I plan on keeping that picture of two hampers standing at the door to show my kids when they're older. It may embarrass them if they're teenagers. But I bet every time God sees it, He'll get a good laugh. He'll have fun with it. And I will too.

Go, eat your bread with joy, and drink your wine with a merry heart,
for God has already approved what you do.
ECCLESIASTES 9:7, *ESV*

REFLECTION QUESTIONS

1. Is your home a fun place to be? Why or why not? What might you need to change to make it more fun?

2. Fun is God's gift to us. What are some new ways you and your family can enjoy God's gift?

45

Helping Mommy

The playroom was a mess. Again. Big sigh. Lindsey and Jessica had been playing baby dolls, and they'd left the dolls, their entire tiny wardrobes and a boatload of accessories spread all over the floor. Apparently, their babies had been hungry, too, because the play food and dishes were mixed in with all the clothes, pacifiers and diapers.

"Lindsey! Jessica!" I called. "Come here, please!"

Lindsey trotted in soon afterward, followed by her sister. "You girls need to clean up the dolls and food and dishes and stuff," I said.

"*All* of them?" Lindsey asked.

"You made a mess with all of them, so now you have to clean all of them up," I explained reasonably. "I'll help you get started."

I knew I could do the job myself in a fraction of the time it would take me to instruct them in how to do it. I also knew they needed to learn to clean up their own messes. So I took a deep breath and determined to be patient. "Okay," I said. "First, Lindsey, you pick up all the dolls. Jessica, you pick up all the clothes for the dolls."

As it turned out, I was right. The job that would have taken me 5 minutes to complete on my own took us 20 minutes to do together. But I was glad I'd required them to help me, because while it hadn't been an efficient use of time for anyone in the short term, it would benefit all of us in the long term.

God asks us to help Him with His work for a similar reason. It's not that He couldn't accomplish His plans for the world without us. He doesn't need our help. The reason He asks us to help Him is so *we* can benefit.

I imagine God could certainly get things done a lot more smoothly and quickly if He didn't have sinful humanity to contend with. If He just spoke and made things happen instead of waiting on us to seek Him and understand what He was trying to communicate to us, most things would get done much more quickly and correctly. Yet He allows us to participate with Him in His work so that we can receive the benefits of doing so.

What are the benefits of participating with God in His work? For starters, we get to do something together. We get to be with Him, carrying out what He wants to happen, and rejoicing in the success of His plans. True, sometimes our interests aren't the same as God's. We don't always care about what He cares about. Sometimes, when He assigns us to a particular task, we balk. We grumble. We don't care that we get to be with Him in His work, because we don't want to be doing His work. We want to do something else. But that doesn't mean that getting to work with Him isn't a privilege. It just means we don't see it because our attitude's all wrong. If we were to regard every task God asked us to do as a privilege, how much different would our attitudes be, even when doing the things we don't like?

A second benefit of doing God's work is that we get to feel competent and useful. As He enables us to accomplish more and more for Him, we become more and more skilled at doing the things He asks of us. We gain a sense of satisfaction from increasing our abilities and using them as they were meant to be used. And we feel valuable because we know we're doing something God considers worthwhile. You see, Mom, God never asks us to do something insignificant. Every service He wants done is valuable to Him, or He wouldn't waste His time or ours assigning us to do it.

That brings us to the third benefit of carrying out God's assignments: we get to know that we are doing something valuable for others. We matter in this world, even if others don't know our name or don't realize that what we did is any big deal. For example, I don't know who set up the chairs for church this morning, but I'm sure glad they did it. And I think the kids pretty much took it for granted that I put lunch on the table, but I know they're glad I did that.

So with all those benefits, why wouldn't we be excited about doing the things God wants us to do? Okay, honestly, some things aren't particularly pleasant. I don't get much joy from changing a really stinky diaper or cleaning up after a sick child. But I have a choice. I can either focus on the negative aspects of the task, the ones I don't enjoy, or I can focus on the truths that I am God's co-laborer even in the less-than-pleasant things, that I'm doing something valuable for God, and that I'm doing something that matters to others.

I'll bet if I took the latter perspective, it would make a big difference. I'll bet my joys would become greater and my complaints fewer. So maybe that's a fourth benefit of joining God willingly in His work. And that makes four more than He has to give me at all.

There is nothing better for a person than that [she] should eat and drink and find enjoyment in [her] toil. This also, I saw, is from the hand of God.
ECCLESIASTES 2:24, *ESV*

REFLECTION QUESTIONS

1. Do you think of what you do as a mom as participating with God in His work?

2. How might it encourage you if you began thinking of your service that way?

46

I'm Done

It was 6:30 in the morning. The campground was quiet.

We were at a family reunion of my husband's mother's side of the family at a small Baptist campground in East Texas. The one dormitory was divided in half, with one side for men and one for women. I was sleeping on the ladies' side with our two girls (Jessica wasn't born yet).

As a child, Kenny could have slept with me on my side, but he wanted to sleep with Daddy. So he and my husband were in the other half of the building.

The way my husband tells it, he was lying there in a deep sleep. He'd gotten to bed late because he'd stayed up talking with family members he hadn't seen in a while, and then he hadn't slept well. So when 6:30 arrived, he was dead to the world.

Phil had taken two mattresses from the beds and laid them side by side on the floor, because there was no easy way to make sure Kenny wouldn't fall out of his bed during the night and hit the hard cement floor. Kenny's mattress was pushed up right next to Phil's. So their faces were only inches from each other when, at 6:30, Kenny suddenly shot straight up in bed, startling my husband wide awake. "I'm done," Kenny said loudly, and scrambled off his mattress in search of breakfast.

My poor husband had to lie there for a while, calming his racing heart, before he could get up and help Kenny find his way to the dining hall.

In Kenny's mind, he was done sleeping, so it was time to get started on the day. At the age of three, he really didn't care whether other people were done or not. *He* was ready to go, and it never occurred to him that other people might not be.

A self-centered focus is understandable for a three-year-old. Expected, even. But it's pretty much assumed that by the time we're adults, we will have gotten over it.

The only thing is, well, we don't always get over it. Even as moms, we remain self-centered long past the time when it might be considered amusing for us to do so. Despite the fact that we now have a husband and children, we may continue to make ourselves the center of our attention.

But I spend all day taking care of the kids, the house, and my husband, we protest. *How can I possibly be called self-centered?*

Maybe it's like this. The kids are acting up, and your husband is sitting at the table reading the morning paper, oblivious. *Why do I always have to handle the discipline around here?* you grumble inwardly.

Or you find an empty glass with the dregs of who-knows-what in the bottom underneath your daughter's bed, and you think, *Am I the only one who can put dirty dishes where they belong? What am I, their* slave?

Or—and I must admit I'm guilty of this one too often—your child does something, and you scold her or discipline her, not because what she did was all that bad, but because *it annoyed you.*

Yikes. It's pretty easy as a mom to be self-focused even while we think we're being others-focused. And it's even easier to try to train that quality out of our children while failing to recognize it in ourselves. Jeremiah 17:9 says, "The heart is deceitful above all things… who can know it?" (*KJV*). I'd say that pretty much sums it up.

So what do we do? How can we make sure our focus is correct when we might not even realize it's wrong?

We do the same thing a growing child does: we rely on someone more mature and more objective than ourselves to point it out to us. Occasionally, someone else in our life will actually be willing to do that. But even when others are afraid to do it, or don't recognize the problem, God always does. And He's always willing to speak words of truth into our life, even when they're not particularly pleasant to hear.

No one likes to hear when she's wrong, especially when it involves something like being self-centered. But it's a result of the Curse that we're out of proper relationship with others. We focus too much on ourselves and what we believe is for *our* good, and we neglect our neighbors. We fail to consider them as more important than we are. In fact, we often fail to consider our neighbors at all, except when they do something we don't like.

But the Bible tells us that we're to have the same attitude Jesus had, and even though He was God, He was most certainly not arrogantly self-centered. In fact, He came not to be served, but to serve. And that's the way we're supposed to be too.

So the first step in becoming like Jesus is to repent of our sins that make us not like Him. Let's repent of putting ourselves at the center of our universe and not treating others of God's children the way He wants them to be treated. But let's go a step further. Let's also ask for His discerning help in pointing out the ways of our heart to us, and where we go wrong.

It won't be an easy thing to do. But if it makes us more like Him, isn't it worth it?

Do nothing out of selfish ambition or vain conceit, but in humility consider others better than yourselves. Each of you should look not only to your own interests, but also to the interests of others. Your attitude should be the same as that of Christ Jesus.

PHILIPPIANS 2:3-5

REFLECTION QUESTIONS

1. Do you tend to focus more on yourself or on others? What does this look like in your life?

2. Do you need to work on putting others first? What are some ways you can do this?

47

Traveling with Jill

One year for our anniversary, my husband and I bought a GPS (global positioning system). We sought recommendations from a friend who's used them all over the world, and we found a really good sale on the brand he recommended. And so it happened that we found ourselves the proud new owners of a small box with a voice that told us how to get almost anywhere we might want to go.

At first, we marveled at the new-to-us technology. ("Wow, isn't that neat? It got us *right here*!" or "Hee hee, we made it say 'route re-calculation' again.") We've had it for four years now, and though I still don't entirely understand how to use it, it's practically a member of our family now. It even has a name: Jill. It's a long, mostly irrelevant story about why it's named Jill, so I'll spare you. But suffice it to say that this device is now a regular part of our lives.

As the novelty has worn off, though, I've started to notice some things about it that annoy me. For one thing, Jill often says something like, "In 100 feet, prepare to exit onto I-20 westbound." Then, as I'm on the entrance ramp, she says, "In 400 feet, prepare to enter I-20 westbound." (What else could I do at this point?) "In 100 feet, merge onto I-20 westbound." ("Okay, okay, already!")

Sometimes, she gives me far more directions than I need. But other times, she doesn't give me enough information until the last minute. The other day, I was driving on a different highway. I knew the exit was coming up soon and, sure enough, Jill pointed that out. "In one mile, prepare to exit onto I-30."

Okay, but then am I going to go east or west? It was fortunate that I had some idea where I was going, because Jill didn't tell me until the last minute. So it turned out not to be that big a deal. But what if I hadn't known where I was going? What if I had had to depend on Jill for information, and she hadn't told me in time to make what I felt was a good decision about which way to travel? What if I hadn't been able to get to the proper lane in time because I hadn't had enough time to prepare?

I hate not having enough time to make decisions when I'm driving. What's even worse is not having enough time to make decisions in life.

I like to plan things out in advance. I don't enjoy having to make last-minute decisions on anything that might be even halfway important. I'd rather know what's coming up and when a decision will be necessary so I can have what I deem sufficient time to decide what I want to do about it, without being under pressure.

Unfortunately, life doesn't always work that way. Issues arise and sudden decisions have to be made. Sometimes that's a problem, because I can't always make an on-the-spot decision. How do I know what's right? I can't see the ultimate outcome of all this, so how do I know what to choose now? And there's no time to decide.

Fortunately, there is Someone who knows exactly what to do in any and every situation, no matter how last-minute it may seem to us. In fact, He's known since eternity past.

God knows every circumstance we'll face in our lives. He knows which ones will look confusing to us and leave us uncertain as to which direction to go. And if He doesn't give us as much advance direction as we'd like, we can be sure there's a reason. But we can also be sure that He *will* tell us in time for us to make the choice He wants us to make. He knows whether He wants us to go east or west, and He'll tell us, if we just ask. After all, He doesn't want us to go the wrong direction any more than we do, and maybe even less.

It turned out that Jill told me which way to turn in plenty of time. I needn't have worried. I could have trusted her. And if a small, man-made computer is worthy of my confidence, how much more is God worthy? After all, Jill made a mistake once. But God has never made a mistake, and He never will.

So trust Him to tell you what you need to do, in time for you to do it. When things are getting down to the wire, or a deadline is closing in, don't get anxious. God knows how much time is left, and He knows how much time you need in order to act. He'll tell you when it's time, and probably not before.

Oh, and by the way . . . I went west.

Whether you turn to the right or to the left, your ears will hear
a voice behind you, saying, "This is the way; walk in it."
ISAIAH 30:21

REFLECTION QUESTIONS

1. Do you like to have everything laid out in advance so you can have time to make your decision, or do you prefer to "fly by the seat of your pants"? Is this ever a problem for you? How might it be an advantage to you?

2. How does your natural inclination about how much advance information you need pertain to how you are able to trust God?

48

Leaning Back

Why do kids love getting dirty but hate getting clean? Most kids I know seem to love dirt. In fact, the muddier they are, the better. Most of them also love being in the bathtub, as long as they don't have to do anything more than sit in the water and play with their toys. But the minute you reach for the soap, it's a different story.

Once, when Ellie was about four, I was attempting to wash her hair. I needed to pour water over her head, but she wouldn't lean back. With my hand on her forehead, I kept trying gently to force her head back far enough so I could pour the water over her without getting any in her eyes. But "gently" wasn't working. She resisted me with all the strength in her little neck. "Ow! Ow!" she screamed.

"Ellie, if you wouldn't resist me, it wouldn't hurt," I said. "You have to bend your neck."

"But it hurts!"

"If you lean your head back, it won't hurt," I said, my patience wearing thin.

"I *am* leaning back."

"You're not leaning back *far enough*."

Hmm. Sounds like me sometimes.

Not that I have a problem with having my hair washed. But at times, I resist God in the same way Ellie resisted me. Let me explain.

God knows exactly what is necessary to accomplish His goals for my life. Sometimes that means He needs me to bend a certain way. But when He starts to bend me, I resist, because it's uncomfortable or it hurts—or maybe just because I'm stubborn and want things my way.

If I don't listen to Him at first, He uses more pressure, and I protest. "But, God, it hurts!" I say, as if He isn't aware of that fact. Or what's worse, I insist that I *am* complying, as if He should be satisfied with my level of compliance.

But we're not the ones to determine when we've bent far enough. We can't always see God's ambitions for us; and even when we can, we don't always understand what's necessary in order to reach those goals.

Apparently, God had this problem with the Israelites, too, because several times in the Bible, He calls them "stiff-necked." He was trying, figuratively speaking, to cleanse them and, as we say in Texas, "They weren't havin' none of it." But their stiff necks were merely outward physical signs of the inner condition of their hearts. Their hearts were rebellious against Him, resulting in their refusal to comply with His directions.

Good thing we moms never have that problem. Oh, wait . . . we do. At least, if you're like me, you do. We get so used to running our home (and, if we are career women, our office) that we become pretty independent. We can do just fine running things on our own, thank you very much. When someone else tries to help us out—even God—we don't see His offering as needed instruction. We resent it as unnecessary interference.

So bending is hard, even when it's something relatively small. But when the issue is huge, it's even more difficult. Sometimes, when we're grieving, and it seems as if God is forcing us to bend beyond our endurance, we can't see anything good in what is going on. If we're honest, we would trade anything He might be accomplishing in our lives for relief from the pain. But if God has decided to bend us, He's going to do it. Resisting Him won't make us feel any better. In fact, it will only make things worse.

If only we would realize that He'll let us straighten up as soon as He can, we'd act a lot differently under the pressure. When I was done washing Ellie's hair, I didn't continue to hold her head back. I allowed her to come upright, and her temporary torment was over. Likewise, God won't ask us to bend any longer than necessary. We can, and should, look forward to the day when He will take the pressure off and we'll begin to rise.

For that time *will* come. And who knows? It just might come sooner if we're willing to bend when God first asks us to do it.

"For my thoughts are not your thoughts,
neither are your ways my ways," declares the LORD.
ISAIAH 55:8

REFLECTION QUESTIONS

1. Is God asking you to bend? In what areas?

2. When God asks you to bend, do you submit or do you fight Him? Why? What needs to change?

49

You're the Greatest

To hear my children tell it, I'm the greatest mom in the world. Okay, so it depends on when exactly you ask them. If it's right after I've made them clean their rooms, they might not agree as readily. But when their hearts are full of love, they're quick to express their feelings.

Lindsey went through a stage for a while when her affirmations of me always seemed to come when I'd just done something for her or given her what she wanted.

"Mommy, may I pwease have a snack?" she would ask.

"Sure," I'd say.

"Mommy, you're the best mommy in de whoh wohld."

Or she'd ask me to go outside and play with her, and I'd agree. "Mommy, you're the gweatest," she'd say.

I'm glad she thinks I'm a great mom. But I hope she thinks so all the time, not just when I've made her happy. I hope her belief that I'm the best mommy in the world doesn't fluctuate depending on how happy she is with what I've done. I love to hear her say I'm the "gweatest" even when it doesn't involve getting something—when it's just because she loves me.

I bet God likes hearing us tell Him He's the greatest too. In fact, I *know* He does. The Bible says that He inhabits the praise of His people. With all the places He could choose to dwell, He chose our praises. He must love hearing them, and feel at home there.

When it comes to praising God, we usually make one of two errors. The first is failing to praise Him enough. Praising God usually isn't high on our priorities list. We're perfectly willing to thank Him when He does something we like, but praising Him? Are we really supposed to spend time telling Him how great He is?

In a word, yes. It's not because He doesn't know He's great. It's because *we* need to spend time contemplating His greatness. Most of us can't remember the last time we spent more than a second or two exalting His virtues. We figure that singing praise choruses in church ought to cover it. But it doesn't. It's far too easy to get lost in singing words we know by heart and not really think about them. Even if we do sing the song from our heart, and God is pleased, it's still not enough.

Why? I think of it this way. Recently, my kids performed in a Mother's Day program at their preschool. They all stood in front of the moms in a little group and sang their hearts out. One of the songs was about how great mommies are, and my children looked adorable singing it. But is it enough for me to hear them singing my praises corporately if they never tell me they think I'm wonderful when we're alone together?

Of course not. Neither is it sufficient for God. Yes, He definitely desires the corporate praise of His people. But we can be certain that He desires one-on-One, intimate praise from us, too.

The second error we often make when it comes to praising God is praising Him only when He's just done something wonderful for us. "Thank You for Your gracious goodness, God," I've been known to pray at times like these. "You are so kind and good to me, and so bountifully generous in giving me these blessings I don't deserve." But do I praise Him like this at other times? Or, perhaps more telling, do I praise Him equally even when He's denied me what I want?

God is worthy to be praised all the time. His worthiness doesn't depend on His having just done something for me, or on whether I'm busy that day. He deserves to be praised *all the time*.

So how does a busy mom do that? How does a mom in the midst of ABCs and macaroni and cheese find time to praise God the way He deserves?

I would like to suggest three ways that we can praise Him. They are certainly not the only ways; you may think of better ones. But they are things that any mommy can do, no matter what her circumstances.

First, we can do the daily tasks of our calling as unto the Lord. When we vacuum and make the beds, we can offer these services to Him as praise—maybe even by telling Him that's what we're doing. It may not seem like offering Him much, but no one in the world can do more than offer back to God what she's been given. If we are offering Him the best we have, that is praising Him.

Second, we can seize small moments here and there to offer Him our words of praise. Young children have an incredible sense of radar, and it seems that whenever we try to sit down with the Lord for any length of time, our children suddenly need us. God understands this. After all, He gave these children to us. And fortunately for us, He accepts brief moments of praise as willingly as He does lengthy praise sessions. And He doesn't count the short ones as substandard, either.

Third, we can play praise music in the background as we go about the rest of our day. When I do this, I often find that a particular phrase jumps out at me just at the moment I need it and inspires me to worship. Plus, there's just something about having Christian music playing that seems to make the day go better. Choose soft instrumentals if you want, or choose Petra. It doesn't matter, as long as you choose what will help you worship the Lord.

Finally, but perhaps most importantly, we can praise God by being completely satisfied in Him. I know that I consider it to be the highest praise when my husband says (despite my many imperfections), "I couldn't have a better wife than you." He is completely satisfied with me, even though I'm not perfect. How much more, then, should I be completely satisfied with God? God's character is filled with infinite goodness and perfection, and there is not the slightest deficiency in Him. Who wouldn't be satisfied with a God like that? Too often, I focus on how satisfied I am with earthly things. But these possessions are nothing more than imperfect foretastes of heaven, and they'll eventually pass away. If I focus on God, however, I will never fail to be completely satisfied. And best yet, He will never pass away. He is wholly satisfying, forever.

I want to make it my goal to praise Him more often. Will you join me in that goal? If so, you will not only bring pleasure to God's heart, which is reward enough in itself, but you'll also experience the incredible blessing of having your heart filled as you praise.

What an amazing God we serve!

I will praise you among all the people; I will fulfill my vows in the presence of those who worship you.
PSALM 22:25, *NLT*

But you are holy, O you that inhabit the praises of Israel.
PSALM 22:3, *AKJV*

REFLECTION QUESTIONS

1. Do you praise God as often as you should? If not, why not?

2. What can you do to make sure you spend more time praising God? What benefits do you think both you and God will receive from your increased praise?

50

Trusting God's Hand

"Hey, Meg? Come look at this," my husband called.

I joined him in the bedroom, where Lindsey was sitting on the floor. "Lindsey marked her hands and feet so she could tell which was which," Phil explained.

I glanced down as Lindsey proudly held up her hands and feet to show me an *L* on one hand and one foot, and an *R* on the other hand and foot, all in black marker. The only problem was . . . she'd gotten it backwards. The *L*s were on the right side, the *R*s on the left. "Hey, good job," I said, deciding to praise the effort rather than the results.

"These will help me wemember which side is wight and which side is weft," Lindsey said.

"I just bet they will," I said. "I love how hard you worked on that."

"Thank you," Lindsey said, pleased.

My husband motioned me to step outside the room, and I joined him in the hall. "I did that for her awhile back," he said in a voice low enough so Lindsey couldn't hear. "I put *L*s and *R*s on her so she could remember which was which. I guess she thought she could do it herself."

Well . . . not quite. I'm sure she figured that because she'd seen Daddy do it once, she could do it easily on her own. But she was mistaken. In this case, it wasn't a big deal. But it can be a much bigger deal when we think we know how to run our lives and go about doing so without consulting God.

There are at least three ways or situations in which we fail to consult God, and therefore run the risk of messing things up by doing them ourselves. The first is when we develop a plan for our lives without regard for what He wants. It's fine to have an idea of where we want to go in life. But before we start trying to make anything happen, we should ask God for His plan. Then we should start working to make His desires come to pass, rather than our own. If our desires are the same as His, great. That's a bonus. But ultimately, if we're trying to implement something God never had in mind, we're doomed either to failure or at least to missing out on many blessings we could have enjoyed otherwise.

We also fail to consult God when we've been through something with Him once before, so we think we know how to do it the second time. That was Lindsey's problem. She had watched Daddy act, so she figured she knew how to do it just as well as he did. When the time came that she needed more letters on her hands and feet, she didn't ask for her daddy's help because she thought she didn't need it. Instead, she tried to help herself. And she messed up. Likewise, we don't ask for God's help when we think we don't need it, and we're often wrong, too.

Then there are the times when we fail to ask God for His help because we think He wouldn't really be interested in helping us. Somehow, we've bought into the idea that "God only helps those who help themselves" as if it were in the Bible—which it's not. We reason that God would expect us to be able to handle certain situations on our own, and we try . . . and fail. So instead of asking for His help at that point, we try harder, because we're afraid that now He might be really disgusted with us for messing up what we should have gotten right the first time.

No, no, no! All three of these are wrong. We are *not* capable of mapping out a blueprint for our own lives. We should *not* decline to consult God just because He helped us with something similar once before. And we do *NOT* serve a God who doesn't want to help us because He'd really prefer that we be more capable on our own. Jesus said that He is the vine and we are the branches, and apart from Him, we can do nothing. Not some things, not many things, but *nothing*. He knows we aren't capable of doing everything on our own. And He died so that we could live in loving relationship with God, with His Holy Spirit living in our hearts to guide us every day, every step of the way.

Let's give up the idea that we can ever be independent from Him, even in the smallest degree. Mom, even our next breath depends on His sustaining power. It's no shame to admit we need help; it's part of being human. And He made us that way because He wanted us to depend on Him for strength, wisdom and guidance. So let's do it. Let's cast ourselves upon Him in full-out dependence, the way He wants us to. And when we get so confused we don't know which way's right and which way's left, let's ask Him. He always knows.

Depend on the LORD *and his strength; always go to him for help.*
1 CHRONICLES 16:11, *NCV*

REFLECTION QUESTIONS

1. Do you try to be independent from God, even in "small" ways? If so, why?

2. What benefits would you receive from depending on God rather than on yourself?

51

Be Thankful

Apparently, candy manufacturers make 1.76 billion candy canes per year. I find that amazing. I mean, I know that well into January, you can still find boxes of candy canes in the clearance cart at the grocery store, but I never realized just how many of them get produced every 365 days.

That staggering number probably explains why a friend of mine had several boxes left over this past year and generously gave us one. Actually, she tried to generously give us several boxes, but I managed to escape with just one. My kids are the only ones in our house who eat candy canes, and I didn't want them ingesting their body weight in sugar.

One day, while I was sitting at the computer, Lindsey came into the room, holding the unopened box. "Mommy, may I pwease give evwybody one?" she asked.

"Sure," I said.

Lindsey walked off. She returned a few minutes later and handed me a candy cane with no wrapper, which she had painstakingly peeled off by herself. "Here you go," she said.

My heart was touched by her sweet gesture, but . . . I don't like candy canes. I hate peppermint. "No thank you, sweetheart," I said. "I don't care for one."

Lindsey thought a second, then looked up at me with her big, solemn brown eyes, and said, "Um . . . be thankful for what I give you."

Yikes. She was right.

"I *am* thankful," I said, and took the candy cane. "Thank you so much."

"You're welcome," Lindsey said, and trotted off to play.

In being caught up in my work, I had totally missed the point. By offering me a candy cane, Lindsey was offering me her heart, too, and she needed to know I accepted it. She needed affirmation not only that her gift was appreciated but that she was valuable.

I'm so glad that God is better at focusing on me and my emotions than I am at focusing on my children. There are times when I hear my kids' words and miss their heart, or when I'm so tired or busy it's hard to focus on anyone but myself. But God never fails to see through my words to what's in my heart. He is never unaware of my needs. And He's certainly never too tired or busy to pay attention to me.

That's amazing when we stop to think about it. It's absolutely incredible that God should care about us at all. The psalmist asks, "What is man that you are mindful of him, the son of man that you care for him?" (Ps. 8:4). God is certainly not obligated to love us. Yet out of His infinite goodness, He chooses to do it. Wow!

As if that weren't enough, God is intimately acquainted with all of our emotions and our needs. He knows what we feel and what sort of response we need. He knows exactly how to minister to us, whether it involves a touch from His Holy Spirit, or prompting a friend to call us, or something else we never would have thought of.

Not only that, but He also invites us to bring all our cares to Him. *All* of them—any emotion, any trial, any confusion. Why? According to the Bible, it's because He cares for us. It's not a matter of reporting our concerns to God and asking Him to do something about them, as if it were some kind of business transaction. It's the natural function of an intimate relationship between God and each of us. We bring our cares to Him because we love Him and we know He loves us. He responds because He knows exactly what we need, and because He loves us.

Too often, we take the extraordinary relationship we enjoy with Him for granted. He provides for us so well that we get used to His gifts and start expecting them. Somehow, we fail to appreciate what He gives, and we begin to accept blessings from His hand without allowing them to turn our hearts toward the Giver.

When He gives me something, I want to delight His heart by thanking Him for it. After all, I love to hear gratitude from my children, and God loves to hear it from His children too. I want God to love giving me gifts, not because I want more stuff but because I want to delight His heart the same way Lindsey's heart would have been delighted if my immediate response to her offering had been thanksgiving. When He thinks about blessing me in some way, I want His heart to be gladdened by the thought of how I will react.

There's something else I want to learn to do, too. I want to see God's heart behind everything He gives me. Just as Lindsey was giving me her gift out of love for me, so too God blesses us because of His love for us. He doesn't do it out of some sense of obligation (as if He is obligated to us for anything). He does it because He loves us. When He gives me something, I want to receive not only the obvious blessing, but also the expression of His love. How beloved would we feel if we learned to see everything God gives us as gifts given out of love? We'd realize that He showers His love upon us, moment by moment, every single day.

That, dear Mom, is the real gift. Anything else is extra.

I will sing unto the LORD, because he hath dealt bountifully with me.
PSALM 13:6, *KJV*

REFLECTION QUESTIONS

1. Is your heart content with what God gives you, or do you often want more?

2. Do you recognize God's heart of love for you behind every way He blesses you?

52

Covering Her Eyes

As I was opening the lunch meat drawer in the refrigerator, I found . . . *it*. A package of cheddar cheese slices with the side slit open. Never mind the fact that the package came with a handy little zipper you could use to reseal the remaining slices when you were done. No, it was the *other* side that was open.

Detective that I am, I deduced that someone must have gotten a snack and been unable to manage the zipper. I narrowed my eyes and calculatedly eyed the only two children in the kitchen. Lindsey and Jessica looked up at me innocently.

"Who wrecked my cheese?" I asked.

Immediately, Lindsey covered her eyes, and I knew I had found the culprit.

Her reaction struck me as amusing. At four years old, she must have known that I could still see her. But she didn't want to see me, and she didn't want to be seen. So she "hid."

Adam and Eve tried the same strategy in the Garden of Eden. First, the serpent deceived Eve, and she ate the forbidden fruit. Then Eve gave some to Adam, and he decided to go ahead and eat it too, even though he knew better. And suddenly . . . they knew they were naked.

I imagine that must have been an interesting realization for them. After all, there was no one else around wearing clothes for them to compare themselves to. None of the animals wore anything other than their skin, fur, feathers or scales. So Adam and Eve probably didn't even realize they needed any clothing.

And they didn't need any—at least not until they sinned.

All of a sudden, something had changed, and they knew it. They were well aware they'd disobeyed God, and they must have realized that something was now horribly wrong. The first thing they wanted to do was hide. The Bible says they wanted to hide themselves from God's face. So they made themselves coverings out of fig leaves.

I imagine they were crouching down behind a bush when they heard the Voice. "Where are you?"

The Bible doesn't tell us, but I'm pretty certain they didn't pop up from behind the bush and say, "We're over here!" Adam does answer, but I'll bet God had to call him more than once. I mean, they were hiding, right? They didn't want to be seen.

Viewed from thousands of years later, their attempt to hide seems silly. *Well, of course God knew where they were,* we think. *Why bother hiding?*

But do you know what? We do the same thing to God. We disobey Him, and then we try to hide.

Most of us aren't going to hide behind a bush while God calls to us. But we do hide in other ways, and we do ignore His voice.

One of the two primary ways we hide from God is deciding not to think about Him. I remember a time in college when I wasn't walking very closely with the Lord. Oh, I wasn't out robbing banks or doing drugs, but I was going my own way, and I knew it. So, during that time, I simply didn't think about Him much. Whenever I did, I felt convicted, and I wasn't interested in that. So I decided not to think about Him. It's much easier to go our own way if we don't think much about how God is probably displeased with us.

The second primary way we hide from God is refusing to listen to His Word. Maybe we stop going to church or refuse to read our Bibles. We try to distance ourselves from anything related to God because, after all, we're trying to hide from Him, right? Or maybe we simply ignore God's Holy Spirit speaking to us. We know good and well that we've done something wrong, but we don't want to hear about it, so we don't listen. We let Him keep calling us, and we don't answer, hoping He doesn't go to the trouble of finding us behind the bush and that He just goes away.

What we don't like to think about is what Lindsey and Adam and Eve didn't want to recognize—God can still see us. Even when we think we're hiding from Him, we're not, because He knows exactly where we are. We're no more hidden from Him than Lindsey was hidden from me when she covered her eyes. Yes, we make it more difficult for Him to talk to us, but we're not hidden.

Since we can't succeed at hiding, we might as well just come clean about whatever it is that we've done. God already knows it anyway. Do we really think that just because we refuse to acknowledge it before Him, He doesn't know our sin, or it hasn't happened? Do we assume that if we can avoid talking about it, we can avoid receiving consequences for it?

We dread acknowledging our sin to God because we're ashamed of having it out in the open. But guess what? It's already in the open. It's the elephant in the living room that we don't want to talk about, but it's right there. God knows it, and we know it, and we're still going to get consequences for it. So let's just admit it and get it dealt with. Then we can truly move on—not as a fugitive on the run who's desperate not to be found out, but as a confident, dearly beloved child of God who knows she's been washed clean.

It's one of the benefits Jesus' death bought us. We don't have to try to hide (as if we really could, anyway). We can confess our sin and know that God will forgive us, cleanse us, and let us start over.

It's the difference between hiding behind bushes and walking openly in the garden. And I'd rather avoid spending most of my life crouched down behind the shrubbery, wouldn't you?

If we confess our sins, he is faithful and just to forgive us our
sins and to cleanse us from all unrighteousness.
1 JOHN 1:9, *ESV*

REFLECTION QUESTIONS

1. When you sin, do you talk to God and willingly confess, or do you hide behind the shrubbery? Why?

2. Is there anything you need to confess to God right now?

53

I Forgive You

If you want to meet the biggest train fan in the world, you should come meet my son, Kenny. He absolutely loves to play with his train sets. He has several different ones that are made out of wood, plastic or metal. One of his favorite things to do with them is to construct complicated swirls and loops of track, add a few plastic trees and stop signs, and build a town. His towns cover approximately the square footage a real city covers, and they're usually spread out in the middle of the kitchen floor or a high-traffic area.

Most of the time, I'm willing to step around them. I love watching Kenny create what he sees in his imagination and hearing him give his trains personalities and act out storylines.

One day, Kenny was sitting on the floor playing, his wooden train set spread out around him. His sisters were off in another part of the house amusing themselves with some game of their own that apparently, from the sounds of it, involved lots of dashing around and giggling. I was working on the computer a few feet away from Kenny when I suddenly heard Lindsey's running footsteps. She darted into the room and right into the middle of Kenny's train set, paused, looked both ways, then turned and ran back the other direction.

"Hey! You stepped on my toy!" Kenny said.

Lindsey didn't hear him. She was already on her way back to her own game.

Kenny waited briefly for her response, but there was none. So he called after her, "I forgive you!" and went back to his trains.

What a great way to resolve the situation. Kenny knew Lindsey had committed an offense against him, and he knew that when someone sins against you, forgiveness needs to be asked for and extended. But because Lindsey was no longer around to apologize, he forgave her *in absentia* and moved on.

It didn't matter to him that Lindsey didn't realize she needed forgiveness, or that she hadn't asked. In fact, he didn't forgive Lindsey for Lindsey's benefit. He did it for his own benefit, so that he would be free to put the incident behind him.

Sounds like something we all need to do. Unlike Kenny, we often hold on to our "right" to be recompensed—or at the very least, apologized to—for offenses that just aren't that big a deal in the grand scheme of things. We insist that other people make things right with us before we can forgive them because, after all, they *owe* us. And we don't want to let them get away with anything.

But if that's the way we feel, we don't really understand what forgiveness is. Forgiveness is *not* saying that what the other person did was okay. It's *not* saying the offense didn't matter. It's certainly not giving the person a license to hurt us again, or even necessarily continuing to spend time around him or her.

Instead, forgiveness is saying that even though we've been sinned against, we're not going to exact a penalty from the offender. We're not saying the person may not deserve to face legal or other consequences. We're simply releasing ourselves from the constant strain of having to be the one to try to collect.

We're acknowledging the same thing Kenny knew—that our ability to forgive doesn't depend upon the other person. It's a decision of our own will. We can remain stuck in the incident, rehashing it over and over in our mind and continuing to stir up our emotions, or we can let it go and set ourselves free.

But how exactly do we let go? Everything in our human nature revolts against the idea. Overlooking an offense doesn't come naturally.

That's why we need God's help. We need Him to show us what letting go looks like. And He did—in the Person of His Son, Jesus. Instead of trying to make people pay for their sins, which He would have had the right to do, Jesus left it up to His Father to collect any penalties for their sin. He Himself continued on the Father's mission, loving the people around Him even when they didn't love Him back, providing a living illustration of God's immense, forgiving love toward us. That's what He wants us to do too.

I know it's far easier said than done. But God is in the business of helping us do what we find impossible. Let's ask Him to increase our trust in Him and make us willing to allow Him to collect on others' debts against us instead of trying to do it ourselves. Let's also ask Him to grant us the willingness to forgive, even when people don't know they need our forgiveness or don't ask for it.

Even when people step on our toy train.

*A [mom's] wisdom gives [her] patience; it is to [her]
glory to overlook an offense.*
PROVERBS 19:11

*When he was reviled, he did not revile in return; when he suffered, he did
not threaten, but continued entrusting himself to him who judges justly.*
1 PETER 2:23, ESV

REFLECTION QUESTIONS

1. Do you have difficulty forgiving others who have hurt you, especially if they don't apologize?

2. Does understanding what forgiveness does and does not mean help you to be able to forgive more easily?

3. Ultimately, why should we forgive offenses against us?

54

What Is That?

Does your front porch tend to get a little cluttered? Mine does. We're blessed with a large front porch, and the same principle seems to operate there that also pertains to purses—the bigger it is, the more stuff you absolutely have to store on or in it.

At any given time, our porch holds four bicycles; a tricycle; a large box of chalk that works wonderfully on the porch and the steps; two chairs; a large end table; and a small end table. I realize we could store these things elsewhere, as we have plenty of space. But it seems much more convenient to keep them on the front porch for easy access.

Usually, I do a pretty good job of keeping all our stuff nice and neat. But on one particular night, as the kids and I were returning from the Y, *something* was up there. Our porch light was out, so everything was dark. And in the darkness, Ellie spotted an unfamiliar shape. "What is that?" she asked, stopping still and pointing.

I followed her finger with my gaze to see what she was looking at. For a moment, I couldn't tell what it was either. But as I stared at it, the shapeless lump became familiar. "It's just my umbrella," I said.

"Oh," Ellie said. "Whew."

"Things do look scary when you don't know what they are," I empathized.

Don't they, though? I don't know about you, but I'm not too wild about the unknown. I don't like it when I have to enter a situation where the details are a little murky—or completely invisible. The unknown can be pretty scary to me. I'm much more comfortable getting everything spelled out and nailed down in advance, so I know exactly what's involved in a situation and what's likely to happen.

Don't get me wrong—I sometimes love to fly by the seat of my pants. In the right kind of situation, I've even been known to find that exhilarating. It all depends on the circumstances. But when I'm not certain about the outcome in a particular arena, or when I'm afraid that a negative outcome is all too likely, I want more details so I can have some kind of control over what's going on. I want to make sure nothing bad happens. I want to protect myself and my loved ones from anything I see as negative.

But I've learned—sometimes willingly, often grudgingly—that I'm never going to have *all* the details. There is only one Person who has them all, and I'm not that Person. He will allow me to have some of the details, as He sees fit, but He's never going to tell me everything.

Even Jesus, when He walked the earth, wasn't privy to all His Father's plans. For example, when His disciples were questioning Him about when the end of the world would come, He replied that no one knows the exact day or hour, not even He, but only the Father. So if God the Father wanted even Jesus to walk in relationship with Him without having all the answers, I should expect that He wants the same from me.

And even if God did tell me everything He knows, my limited human brain wouldn't be able to keep track of it all, much less understand and make use of it. I'd probably take the pieces of information I could grasp and use them as seemed best to me, and in the process make a mess of everything. Too much information in the hands of a person who lacks wisdom and discernment in how to use it is almost never a good thing.

Instead of spending my time and energy trying to figure everything out, I'd do much better to rely on God to tell me what I need to know and guide me through the rest. Often, I won't know as much as I want to know. But I'll always know as much as I *need* to know. After all, God cares deeply about me and wants me to be able to complete the works He's prepared in advance for me to do (see Eph. 2:10). He's not going to withhold information from me that is truly necessary to my success in those things to which He's called me.

Another facet of this truth, which can be difficult to accept, is that sometimes our *not* knowing serves God's purposes better in a situation that our knowing would. Maybe we need to learn to rely more on God and walk by faith, not by sight. Maybe God intends that our character be developed. Maybe we'll never know His purpose, because it's not something that would ever occur to us. But we can know that He does have a purpose, and that His purposes are always good.

Next time we find ourselves facing a situation we don't completely understand, instead of jumping in feet first and frantically trying to manage it ourselves, let's stop and take a deep breath. Let's remember that God understands the situation completely. He knows all the details, and He'll tell us exactly what we need to know in order to cope.

For even though the situation may look to us like an ominous lump on the porch, God's well aware that it's just an umbrella.

For in the time of trouble He shall hide me in His pavilion; in the secret place of His tabernacle He shall hide me; He shall set me high upon a rock.

PSALM 27:5, *NKJV*

REFLECTION QUESTIONS

1. Are you quick to assume that "lumps on the porch" are threatening, or do you assume that they're merely umbrellas?

2. When you see truly ominous circumstances ahead, do you consult your Father to see whether they're really anything to worry about? Then do you act on what He says?

55

The Proposal

Not too long ago, I received a proposal of marriage.

What makes this especially interesting is that I've been married to my husband for 15 years, and the person who proposed to me knew I was married. But I suppose I can forgive her for her impropriety, since she was only three at the time.

Lindsey has always been my cuddlebug. Her love language is definitely physical touch. She enjoys cuddling, hugs and kisses, and even being tickled. She'll bounce into my lap, wrap her arms around me, and squeeze with all her might. Each night, *she* gives *me* a "goodnight hug and kiss."

She also frequently expresses her love with words. For example, just yesterday she said, "Mommy, I'll never stop loving you."

"And I'll never stop loving you," I responded.

"But I'll miss you when you die," she said.

Fortunately, I'm pretty sure I'm in good health, so as far as I know, my death won't be taking place anytime soon.

It was a few months before that when she proposed to me. Lindsey came into the room where I was working, poked her head around the corner, and said, "Mommy?"

I turned my attention to her, and she smiled shyly. "Do you want to marry me?" she asked.

"Aw, sweetie, I'd love to marry you," I said. "But I'm already married to Daddy. What are we going to do about that?"

"You can both marry me," she said. "Then we can be together forever."

"That sounds like a great idea," I said.

Her proposal having been accepted, Lindsey climbed into my lap, and I gave her a hug. We cuddled there for a minute, just enjoying being together. I felt loved, and I know Lindsey felt not only loved but also secure. *We'll be together forever.*

The marriage Lindsey was suggesting will never take place on this earth. But someday, if she comes to know and love God, and to accept Jesus into her life as her Lord and Savior, we'll all be together in heaven. Forever. And there, an even better marriage will take place, one that will last for eternity.

Heaven is not merely a place where we go to sit on clouds and strum harps. It's definitely not an ages-long church service. It's a place we'll be more alive than ever before, and where each of us, whether single, married, divorced or widowed on this earth, will become a bride—the bride of the Lamb.

In heaven, God will prepare an elaborate wedding feast, and it will be for us as we become the bride of His Son. It will celebrate our marriage to the perfect Husband. Any difficulties we've had in our earthly marriages will seem like nothing, and even the joys we've experienced will be eclipsed by the everlasting joy of being wedded to Jesus, our Savior.

In fact, Jesus has already proposed to us, and if we're Christians, we've already accepted His proposal. We may not have thought of it in these terms, but when His Spirit spoke to our hearts and awakened us to our need for Him, He was proposing marriage. He wants to love us far more intimately and perfectly than even the best earthly marriage, and He wants to be together with us and live with us forever. When we acknowledged our need for Him and asked Him to save us and be Lord of our lives, we accepted His proposal. *Yes,* we said. *Yes, I love You, and I want You in my life forever.*

Have you ever thought about what it will be like to be the bride of Christ? I hadn't, until recently. I knew what the Bible said about the Church's being Christ's bride, but I had never really thought about what that would be like.

The Bible tells us that there is rejoicing in heaven at the marriage that is about to take place. We, the bride, have been given fine clothing to wear, and there is a wedding feast laid ready. We know that our Groom is magnificent, because He is Christ Himself. It's going to be the wedding to top all weddings. Not even the fanciest earthly wedding will hold a candle to this one. And we'll all get to be the bride! Not only beautifully arrayed, but eagerly anticipated, passionately loved, and joyfully honored.

So what does this mean for us today, in the midst of our (probably) quite ordinary lives? It means we have a wedding to look forward to! We may have had a beautiful wedding in the past, but it was only a foreshadowing of what this one will be. And if we spent so much time preparing for and dreaming of a wedding that will last, at the most, 70 or 80 years, how much more should we long for our wedding that is yet to come?

That, my friends, will be a wedding to look forward to!

Then I heard what sounded like a great multitude, like the roar of rushing waters and like loud peals of thunder, shouting: "Hallelujah! For our LORD God Almighty reigns. Let us rejoice and be glad and give him glory! For the wedding of the Lamb has come, and his bride has made herself ready. Fine linen, bright and clean, was given her to wear."... Then the angel said to me, "Write: 'Blessed are those who are invited to the wedding supper of the Lamb!'"

REVELATION 19:6-9

REFLECTION QUESTIONS

1. Does it bring joy to your spirit to know that one day, you will become the bride of Christ and enjoy the best wedding feast ever?

2. Do you spend much time anticipating your coming wedding? If not, why not?

56

Stylin'

Ellie was probably about 21 months old on the day she took her Hello Kitty purse to the park. She had gotten it for Christmas the month before, and she carried it everywhere. It was a small shiny purse made of thick, bright pink vinyl, with Hello Kitty's face in white on the side. Ellie loved that purse. She even slept with it. So when she wanted to take it with us to the park, I agreed.

Kenny was only three months old at the time. I sat on one of the swings with him sleeping in his carrier at my feet while Ellie played. At one point, I checked on Kenny, who was still sleeping peacefully, and adjusted his light blanket. When I glanced up, I saw Ellie trotting across the playground, still holding tightly to the straps of that purse. And in that moment, I realized something that made my heart profoundly sad.

Right now, she's carrying that purse because she *likes the way it looks,* I thought. *When she's a teenager, she'll choose her purse so that* others *will like the way it looks.*

Or maybe she won't. Maybe she'll be so secure in her identity and status as God's dearly beloved child that she won't care what others think. But I suspect that, like the rest of us, she'll struggle with this issue.

I struggled a lot with it as I grew up. I desperately wanted to be considered beautiful and popular. I chose clothing with an eye toward how others would see it, and I tried to style my hair and act in ways that would make me a part of the "in" crowd. I wanted to do everything I could, without crossing certain lines, so people would be impressed with me.

The very thought that in another 10 years, my daughter might be struggling for others' acceptance grieved my heart. I think she's beautiful and wonderful just the way she is. It would make me deeply, profoundly angry and sad if others looked at her and didn't appreciate her just because she didn't have the right kind of purse.

I wonder how God must feel when we treat others that way. I bet it makes Him angry. In fact, He makes the point through the apostle Paul that we are not to treat people differently based on how they look and how much money they have. Why not? Because those things don't matter, and He knows it.

We know how we'd feel if our own children received this kind of treatment. It's easy for us to agree that God is offended when others are treated this way. But we don't often stop to think that God feels the same way when *we* are treated like this. After all, we're His children too. He didn't intend for us to have to struggle for acceptance any more than we want our children to struggle. Yes, in this world, we will have trouble, but that wasn't God's original plan. That's why Jesus commanded us to love each other—because God wants us to treat each other *right*. So we can be like Him, yes, but also so no one has to endure the pain of being brushed aside or looked down upon. Including you and me.

You see, God cares about us. He cares far more than you and I care for our own children. He already thinks we're wonderful, and He wants us to agree with Him. He doesn't want us to allow our sense of value to be determined by others. He wants us to accept *His* estimation of our worth. Yet, too often, we consider others' opinions accurate and God's a biased suggestion. We don't fully believe that He really thinks we're wonderful, or if we do, we assume it's just because He's obligated to have some kind of positive opinion about everybody.

Nothing could be further from the truth. God's not obligated to do anything He doesn't want to do. He's certainly not obligated to flatter us. He knows all truth, and He *can't* lie. So why do we discount His opinion and look to faulty human beings for confirmation?

God couldn't care less about whether we're carrying the right purse. What He cares about is that we're His dearly beloved creations, and that *that's* what determines our value—His assessment of us. It all comes down to whom we're going to believe: the omniscient, omnipotent God of the universe or an imperfect human being who doesn't have any better judgment than we do?

Let's acknowledge that what God says about us is true—we *are* wonderful creations. We have worth, and we're valuable. And that value is completely separate from anything we possess. Our value does not come from our clothes. It's not found in our shoes. And despite what we may think, it's not even found in a shiny, pink Hello Kitty purse.

That kind of purse is fun to take to the park. But it doesn't reflect our value.

This is why I tell you: do not be worried about the food and drink you need in order to stay alive, or about clothes for your body. After all, isn't life worth more than food? And isn't the body worth more than clothes?

MATTHEW 6:25, GNT

REFLECTION QUESTIONS

1. Do you spend more time thinking about whether you're pleasing other people or whether you're pleasing God?

2. Do you treat others equally well no matter what their position in life?

57

I Found You!

I loved playing hide-and-seek as a child, but I love it even more now that I'm an adult. That's because now, I always get to be the "finder," since the kids always want to be the ones to hide. Being the finder in a game of hide-and-seek with toddlers and preschoolers always makes for some good, silly fun.

"Mommy, let's play hide-and-seek!" somebody suggests. "You be the finder."

"Okay," I say, and cover my eyes with my hands. "One . . . two . . . three . . ." I count loudly and slowly as I hear the giggles and the feet scampering for a good hiding spot.

"Eight . . . nine . . . ten!" I uncover my eyes and open them.

Most of the time, somebody is still working on getting hidden, and it's usually Jessica. One of her siblings will be crouched down behind something, beckoning Jessica into the hiding place, and Jessica willingly follows. But even when she's done hiding, usually one of her hands or feet is still visible.

Oh, and have you noticed how kids always hide in the same places? I remember when Ellie was just getting old enough to play hide-and-seek. She absolutely loved that game. The only thing was, she would hide in the same place 10 times in a row. I always pretended to look for her, though. She would let me look for a while, then step out of hiding and smile at me. "Oh, there you are!" I would say, as if it were a surprise.

Actually, I don't think hiding is the point of the game for young kids. It might become the point when they get older and gain the ability to hide in some really hard-to-find places. But when they're young, the point of the game is not hiding, but being found. It's not very satisfying to stay hidden for so long that it takes Mommy forever to find them. No, they want to be found, because that's what brings the most joy.

We sometimes treat life like it's a game of hide-and-seek from God. Only we get it backward and think the point is in the hiding. We can easily be deceived into believing that satisfaction is found when we're off by ourselves, out from under God's watchful eye, doing whatever we want to do. We couldn't be more wrong.

Joy is not found in trying to hide from God. In fact, that's what hell is—permanent separation from God. So why would we think that any degree of separation from Him would be the best part of what we're looking for?

If only we realized about our lives what our kids know about hide-and-seek: the best part of the game is *being found*. My kids absolutely love it when I find them. They smile and laugh and pop out of their hiding places, ready to begin the game anew. They're delighted that I looked for them and found them. Secretly, and probably subconsciously, they're glad they couldn't hide so far that I couldn't find them.

What an incredible blessing that we have a God who even wants to look for us. In fact, while we were still sinners, Jesus came seeking the lost. He sought us then, and He seeks us now when we stray from Him. In fact, Jesus told a parable about how much God rejoices over the return of a lost sheep (see Luke 15:3-7).

But that's where the analogy between the game of hide-and-seek and the course of life ends, for while it's acceptable to try to hide from the finder during a game, it's never right to try to hide from God. In fact, it's quite the opposite. We should be so delighted about being in God's presence that we spend all of our time looking for ways to be with Him instead of trying to hide from Him. We should strive to keep Him within sight, not to hide ourselves so well that while He can still see us, we can no longer see Him.

It's not like we can hide, anyway. Just because we can't see God doesn't mean He can't see us. So let's stop playing the game. Instead of hiding behind the couch with our feet sticking out, let's make every effort to stay in God's presence. And let's remember that joy comes not when we can't see Him, but when we can.

Nothing in all creation is hidden from God. Everything is naked and exposed before his eyes, and he is the one to whom we are accountable.

HEBREWS 4:13, *NLT*

But let the godly rejoice. Let them be glad in God's presence. Let them be filled with joy.

PSALM 68:3, *NLT*

REFLECTION QUESTIONS

1. Do you love that you've been found by God? Do you experience joy in His presence? Why or why not?

2. Has there ever been a time when you tried to hide from God? How did you feel after you returned to His presence?

58

Simply Put

I love it when young children pray. Their prayers are so sweet and innocent. Even when they use the same words or phrases we use, it's sweet because they're trying so hard to pray "right." But most times, they come up with prayers that are completely their own.

I still remember Ellie's first prayer. She was about 18 months old. As I put a snack on the high chair tray in front of her, she bowed her head, clasped her little hands, and said, "Myna, myna, myna, myna. Amen." I loved it! I still don't know exactly what she said, but I bet God did.

Then there was the time Kenny wanted to pray at the dinner table, but he wasn't sure exactly what to say. We all bowed our heads and closed our eyes. "Dear God," he began. When he didn't continue right away, I opened my eyes and glanced at him. His head was still bowed and his hands still clasped, but he was looking sideways at me. "Now what do I say?" he whispered.

A couple months ago, it was Lindsey's turn to pray after we had our Bible lesson. She clasped her hands, bowed her head, and closed her eyes. "Deah God," she prayed earnestly, "I wike You. And I don't wike the devil. In Jesus' name we pway. Amen."

I think that just about says it all, don't you? So simple, yet so profound. I believe her prayer touched the heart of God more than many of the ones I've prayed lately. I bet that's part of what Jesus meant when He said that we must enter the Kingdom as little children. Kids are simple and straightforward. And that's what He wants from us too.

As Lindsey knew, loving God doesn't have to be complicated. Yet we often make it that way. We set up an elaborate list of things we have to do, and do *right*, so we can be sure we're loving God

properly. We think we have to do church in a certain way and offer the right programs. We have to find the right Bible reading
plan. We must join the right committees in church and volunteer
for enough ministries both inside and outside the church to fulfill our "service requirement." We should pray using the right
acrostic; include enough missionaries; and always intercede for
others before we mention ourselves. Oh, and we'd better not forget to enroll our children in all the right children's activities.

Obviously, none of these things is bad in and of itself. Reading
God's Word, participating in ministry, praying for missionaries—
all of these are great. In fact, they are things that are not only good
to do, but also that we are *commanded* to do. So the problem's not
with doing them. The problem comes when we focus more on our
activities than on loving God.

The way God designed it, being a Christian is actually pretty
simple. The Bible says He doesn't require anything of us but to do
justice, to love kindness, and to walk humbly with Him. So the
ways in which we do that are nothing but the means He's given us
through which we can express our love for Him.

Allow me to rephrase the first part of 1 Corinthians 13, right
before the famous "love" passage: "If I speak with all eloquence
when I teach Sunday School, but have not love, I am only a re-
sounding gong or a clanging cymbal. And if I have prophetic pow-
ers, and know exactly what my children are doing, and if I've read
every Christian parenting book on the shelves, but have not love,
I am nothing. If I enroll my children in every church activity that's
offered, and spend my time praying for them while I wait to pick
them up, but have not love, I gain nothing."

Notice that Paul didn't say that doing all these things is the
same as loving God. No, he clearly separated the two. We can do
them as a result of our loving God, or we can perform them without
loving Him at all, or at least, without thinking about loving Him.

Mom, when we get to heaven, God's not going to ask us what
we *did*. He'll ask us if we loved Him. He's not going to ask us how
full our calendar was. He'll ask us if we obeyed His command to
love others.

So let's focus on loving Him, rather than on doing things for Him. Yes, serving Him is important, but it shouldn't be our primary focus. Love for God; love for others. *Those* are the things toward which we should put our efforts. If we get love right, everything else will fall into place.

> *He has told you, O man, what is good; and what does*
> *the LORD require of you but to do justice, and to love kindness,*
> *and to walk humbly with your God?*
> MICAH 6:8, *ESV*

REFLECTION QUESTIONS

1. Do you tend to make being a Christian more complicated than it has to be? If so, in what ways?

2. Would it make a difference in your Christian walk if you began to think of it in terms of loving God and others instead of having to do a bunch of things?

I Made a Star!

I love the smell of Play-Doh. In fact, I'll confess to one of my quirks: whenever I open a canister of Play-Doh for my kids, I smell it before I give it to them. It has rather a heady bouquet of childhood, creativity, and good, wholesome fun, all rolled into one. Personally, I think there should be a plug-in air freshener scented like Play-Doh. I'd plug it in every time I wanted to inspire my kids to be creative instead of complaining that they're bored.

My kids love Play-Doh too. They like to cut shapes out of it, roll it into balls and drop tiny crumbs of it all over the floor (which are too small to see until they've been stepped on and flattened out into bigger, colored circles). For some reason, I don't mind vacuuming it up, even though vacuuming is generally not my favorite household chore. (Neither is laundry, dishes, cleaning the bathrooms and a lot of other things I could name. But that's a whole different story.)

One day, the kids had gotten out the bag full of Play-Doh and accessories. Play-Doh was spread out all over the table in various shapes and sizes. Ellie, Kenny and Lindsey were hard at work creating various animals and other shapes. Jessica sat in her booster seat mashing several colors together into one large, brownish-gray ball.

"Look, Mommy!" Kenny said. He held up a blue . . . something. "I made a star!"

His creation didn't look like a star to me. It more or less resembled a blue sugar cookie gone wrong, a shapeless mass of dough with uneven edges. But as far as Kenny was concerned, it was definitely a star.

"Good star!" I said, and Kenny returned happily to his work.

Was I lying? No. Because it all depends on what it takes to make a good star. Here's what I mean. If it takes perfection, then Kenny's star was most definitely not a good one. But if it takes the best effort a person can give, his was great. Because I chose to count his star good, based on how hard he'd tried, he felt proud. How different things would have been if I had said, "Kenny, that's not a star. Stars have five points, and yours has three. Plus, stars are supposed to be evenly formed all the way around. So that's not a star."

Can you imagine the disappointment and shame that would have crushed my little boy's spirit if I had said that? In the face of such criticism, it would have been completely understandable if he had left the table because he didn't ever want to work with Play-Doh again. Even if he had somehow mustered up the heart to try to make another star, the joy of it would have evaporated. He would have been doing it out of a desperate need for my approval, rather than the joy of sharing his creation with me. That old saying, "Sticks and stones can break my bones, but words can never hurt me" simply isn't true.

Fortunately, God is well aware of this. He knows that our tender hearts need encouragement, not callous criticism, if they are to blossom. He doesn't judge our efforts based on the final outcome, but on the state of our hearts and whether we did our best. And even when He does have to tell us that something is not good, He does it in such a way that He doesn't make us feel worthless or unloved.

As moms, we're far harder on ourselves in this way than He is on us. We often hold ourselves up against a standard of perfection (though even that looks different for each of us) and belittle ourselves when we fall short. We can't accept even our own best efforts if those efforts don't result in the perfection we hope for—or, worse yet, think we *should* be able to attain. Instead of seeing our imperfections as reminders that we are merely human, we take them to heart and feel bad about ourselves.

Moms, let's give ourselves a break and offer our hearts the same grace God gives us. Let's learn to recognize when we've done the best we can and be satisfied with that.

After all, God says our star is good enough, and He knows everything. Shouldn't we agree with Him?

A father is tender and kind to his children. In the same way, the Lord is tender and kind to those who have respect for him.
PSALM 103:13, *NIRV*

REFLECTION QUESTIONS

1. Do you primarily look at the degree of "perfection" of what your children achieve or at their efforts?

2. Does God give you more grace in terms of getting perfect results than you give yourself?

Are We There Yet?

It had been a long week for all of us, and the end still wasn't in sight. We had spent the past several days not only taking care of our regular responsibilities, but also attending Vacation Bible School, with which I had assisted. After the closing program and meal on the last day, we loaded up the van for a long trip out of town. I was dreading the five-hour trip, hoping my tired, cranky kids wouldn't bicker too much on the way. But, miraculously, all of them fell asleep not two miles into the trip. "Let's just keep driving," I said to my husband. So we drove on until the kids began to wake up about two hours later.

"I'm hungry," I heard someone say from the back seat. "I need a snack!"

"We'll be stopping for supper soon," I said.

There was silence for a brief moment as they rubbed some more sleep out of their eyes. Then, *it* came—the question I knew was coming. "Are we there yet?" they asked hopefully.

Green fields stretched on either side of us and ahead of us as far as I could see. On our right was a group of cows. ("Look! Kay-ows!" Jessica shouted excitedly, pointing.) It definitely didn't look like the Houston suburbs, and my sister-in-law's house was no-where in sight. "No, we're not there yet," I said.

It wasn't the last time they asked that question. Between the first time and now, as I type this while my husband drives, they've repeated the question in some form approximately 287 more times. All the versions boil down to, "Are we almost there?"

"Not yet," I always respond. "But we're getting closer."

Who can blame them for asking so often? They're excited. Not only will they get to enjoy spending time with family, but we also have a church reunion with a bounce house and face painting to attend tomorrow. What could be better?

On this earth, maybe nothing, at least as far as they're concerned. But I can think of one thing that'll be far better than the best festivities on earth: heaven. It'll be wonderful beyond our wildest dreams. Yet we spend much more time anticipating vacations than looking forward to going to our eternal dwelling place.

Part of the reason is because the topic of dying is uncomfortable for us. We don't like to think of all the pain and grief associated with death. But perhaps if we were to start anticipating heaven the way we should, there wouldn't *be* so much pain and grief surrounding it. Sure, we'd continue to miss loved ones who've gone before us. Even Jesus cried when one of His friends died (see John 11:35). But if we truly realized what an incredible place heaven is, maybe instead of dreading death or fighting against it, we'd look forward to it as the gateway to a fabulously incredible life that would never end.

In heaven, there will be no more death, mourning, crying or pain. We'll dwell in a place of infinite beauty and perfection, which is full of wonders we've never dreamed of. We will no longer suffer the imperfections of our earthly bodies—disability, food allergies, chronic conditions, or poor eyesight. We'll be able to see loved ones who've died in Christ before us. Best of all, we'll dwell in the immediate, face-to-face presence of God Himself. *Forever.*

Can you even imagine how great that will be? It sure sounds a lot better than houses that won't stay clean, discipline problems that won't stay fixed, and colds that crop up at the worst times. Don't get me wrong; I love being a mom. There's nothing else on earth I'd rather do. But I do look forward to heaven.

I long to live in a place of perfection, in the presence of my Savior, with nothing standing in the way of knowing and loving Him and learning of Him throughout eternity. Wouldn't you love to live in a place like that, too?

The great news is that if you are a Christian, one day you *will* live there. There's no doubt about it. In fact, Jesus is already there, preparing a place specially designed for you. And when the time is right, He'll take you there.

Until then, instead of trying to hang on to this fleeting life with all your strength, spend your time anticipating heaven and the glories that await you. "Are we there yet?" you can ask. And God will say, with a smile, "Not yet. But you're getting closer."

But as it is, they desire a better country, that is, a heavenly one.
Therefore God is not ashamed to be called their God, for he
has prepared for them a city.
HEBREWS 11:16, *ESV*

REFLECTION QUESTIONS

1. Do you look forward to going to heaven? Why or why not?

2. What do you think you will most enjoy getting to experience when you get to heaven? What will you most enjoy being free from?

Afterword

Isn't that an amazing thought—that every moment, we're getting closer to a place where we'll be able to see God face to face and hear Him clearly? No more wondering if He's really present with us. No more difficulty trying to determine what He's saying. No more being desperate for sweet, intimate communion with Him that we can't quite figure out how to make happen. We'll hear His voice because *He will be right there,* and we'll never miss hearing it again.

But in the here and now, before we reach heaven, our spirits still thrive on hearing His voice. I hope these devotionals have shown you how it's possible to hear God in the midst of the very ordinary things of life. I pray you've begun to hear Him more, perhaps even at unexpected times and places.

After all, God is the Master of choosing unexpected times and places to make His message known. Who would have ever predicted the Messiah of Israel would be born in a stable during a census ordered by a Roman conqueror?

Here's the exciting thing: God's message hasn't changed between then and now. Jesus came to earth to spread the great news that humankind could get right with a God who loved them deeply. That's still His message to you. God loves you, and He wants a relationship with you. He would do anything to make that possible, including sending His Son to take the punishment for your sins—the punishment you deserved. But that's not all. He also made His Holy Spirit available to dwell in your heart and minister His love and truth to you all day, every day, for your whole life long.

How do you get that? How do you receive this incredible gift of God's constant, loving presence? You have to humble yourself. You have to admit that you've sinned and fallen short of God's standards. And you have to ask God to forgive you, acknowledge Jesus as your Lord, and invite Him to rule your life.

If you've done that, you can know that you're a Christian. John 1:12 says that everyone who receives Christ is a child of God and that God's Holy Spirit dwells in the heart of every believer. So you know that God will never leave you or forsake you and that, someday, you'll dwell with Him in heaven.

What if you're already a Christian? Perhaps you've been one for a long time, but you don't often hear His voice. It might be that there is some sin in your heart that prevents you from hearing Him and that you need to repent. It may be that He's asking you to walk by faith for a while, without His voice. Or it may be that He's speaking to you in a way you're not used to hearing.

That's why I wrote this book. I wasn't used to hearing Him this way, either—in the dailyness of life, and especially during tasks that didn't seem particularly holy. But God was gracious unto me, a sinner, and began to open my "spiritual ears" to hear.

Why not ask Him to open your spiritual ears so you can hear Him throughout the day? So you can walk with Him in unending fellowship? But I warn you: if you do—if you start hearing Him in the small stuff—your whole world is going to change. That's because after encountering God intimately on a regular basis, you can never be the same.

You'll be taking a risk. You'll be allowing Him to step in and change your spiritual world for the better. Are you willing to take the risk? Are you willing to let Him lead you on an incredible spiritual adventure?

You'll still have diapers and car pools and tantrums to deal with. But instead of being drudgery, they'll be another means to hearing God's voice. Why not let Him redeem the mundane into something beautiful?

I pray that the eyes of your heart may be enlightened in order that you may know the hope to which he has called you, the riches of his glorious inheritance in his holy people.

EPHESIANS 1:18

About the Author

Megan Breedlove is the author of numerous devotionals and articles, both online and in print. With a heart for encouraging moms, Megan is a popular speaker at churches and women's groups. She graduated from Baylor University with a University Scholars degree (with an emphasis in psychology and foreign languages) and from Southwestern Baptist Theological Seminary with dual master's degrees in Marriage and Family Counseling and Religious Education. Megan and her husband, Phillip, reside in Fort Worth, Texas, with their four children, Ellie, 8; Kenny, 6.5; Lindsey, 5; and Jessica, 3. They attend Southfield Christian Fellowship in Arlington. Megan enjoys reading, racquetball, playing the piano, and studying foreign languages. To contact Megan, or to read her weekly uplifting devotionals, visit her website at www.Manna ForMoms.com.

To contact the author, please visit the following:

Website: www.mannaformoms.com.

Email: megan.breedlove@mannaformoms.com.

Facebook: http://www.facebook.com/pages/
Megan-Breedlove/123825034311589

Twitter: http://twitter.com/MeganBreedlove.

God, in His infinite mercy, has called me to encourage moms to glorify and enjoy Him in their daily lives. If your church or mother's group would like to receive that ministry through a personal visit, please contact me. I would love to speak to your group in person.

I consider it a privilege to follow God wherever He leads me, so as such, I do not charge a "speaker's fee." If God has a message He wants your group to hear, and if He wants me to deliver that message, He will provide the finances to make that happen.

So if you would like for me to come speak to your group, my only request is that you please pray for the following things:

- Pray that God will clearly reveal His holy will to you, to me, and to my husband, so we can all join Him in it.

- Pray that God will provide for my travel, lodging, and childcare needs.

- Pray that I will be faithful to hear and to clearly communicate the message God wants me to deliver to your group.

- Pray that your hearts will be prepared to receive the message God gives to me for your group.

I look forward to meeting you and your group!

More Great Resources
for M♥ms

The Coffee Mom's Devotional
Celeste Palermo
ISBN 978.08307.46460

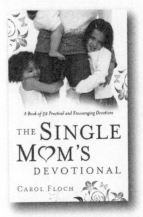

The Single Mom's Devotional
Carol Floch
ISBN 978.08307.51617

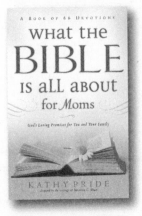

**What the Bible Is All
About for Moms**
Kathy Pride
ISBN 978.08307.51600

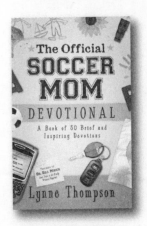

**The Official Soccer
Mom's Devotional**
Lynne Thompson
ISBN 978.08307.45838

The First Prayers Your Baby Will Hear

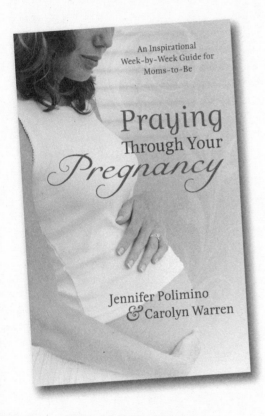

Even before your baby was conceived, he or she was on God's calendar! The heavenly Father has incredible plans for your child, and it is never too early to begin praying for His power and protection over your precious baby's life. *Praying Through Your Pregnancy* is a week-by-week guide for nurturing your baby's spirit as he or she grows within your womb. Each chapter reveals what is happening with your child's development that week, starting with the very first moment of conception. Each week, you'll find a powerful "Mother's Prayer" to guide your conversations with God as well as recommended Scripture meditations so that you can hide His Word in your heart—cultivating your relationship with the Father as your child grows. As your little one develops physically, you'll learn how to place your confidence in God and reduce stress and anxiety as you trust in Him. Draw close to the Creator and get to know His newest creation—your baby—through the power of prayer!

Praying Through Your Pregnancy
Jennifer Polimino &
Carolyn Warren
ISBN 978.08307.48082